THE TRAININGS OF THE PSYCHOANALYST

THE CENTRE FOR FREUDIAN ANALYSIS AND RESEARCH LIBRARY

Series Editors:
Anouchka Grose, Darian Leader, Alan Rowan

CFAR was founded in 1985 with the aim of developing Freudian and Lacanian psychoanalysis in the UK. Lacan's rereading and rethinking of Freud had been neglected in the Anglophone world, despite its important implications for the theory and practice of psychoanalysis. Today, this situation is changing, with a lively culture of training groups, seminars, conferences and publications.

CFAR offers both introductory and advanced courses in psychoanalysis, as well as a clinical training programme in Lacanian psychoanalysis. It can provide access to Lacanian psychoanalysts working in the UK, and has links with Lacanian groups across the world. The CFAR Library aims to make classic Lacanian texts available in English for the first time, as well as publishing original research in the Lacanian field.

www.cfar.org.uk

THE TRAININGS OF THE PSYCHOANALYST

Annie Tardits

Translated by Marc du Ry

KARNAC

First published in 2000 in French as
Les formations du psychanalyste by Annie Tardits, Erès

This edition first published in 2010 by
Karnac Books Ltd
118 Finchley Road, London NW3 5HT

Copyright © 2010 to Annie Tardits

The right of Annie Tardits to be identified as the author of this work has been asserted in accordance with §§ 77 and 78 of the Copyright Design and Patents Act 1988.

Copyright © 2010 to The Centre for Freudian Analysis and Research Library for the translation.

All rights reserved. No part of this publication may be reproduced, stored in a retrieval system, or transmitted, in any form or by any means, electronic, mechanical, photocopying, recording, or otherwise, without the prior written permission of the publisher.

British Library Cataloguing in Publication Data

A C.I.P. for this book is available from the British Library

ISBN 978 1 85575 643 4

Edited, designed and produced by The Studio Publishing Services Ltd
www.publishingservicesuk.co.uk
e-mail: studio@publishingservicesuk.co.uk

www.karnacbooks.com

CONTENTS

ABOUT THE AUTHOR					vii

INTRODUCTION					ix

CHAPTER ONE
The First Analysts					1

CHAPTER TWO
The Berlin Model					19

CHAPTER THREE
The Introduction of Training: Crises and Debates		37

CHAPTER FOUR
From one Training to Another				67

CHAPTER FIVE
The Training of the School				91

CHAPTER SIX
The Apparatuses of the School   121

REFERENCES AND BIBLIOGRAPHY   151

INDEX   161

ABOUT THE AUTHOR

Annie Tardits studied Philosophy at the École Normal Superieure. She is a Freudian psychoanalyst practicing in Paris. She has published a number of studies on psychoanalytic theory and practice and on psychoanalysis and artistic creation, in particular her paper in *Joyce and Lacan*, edited by Jacques Aubert, and a paper on psychoanalysis and anthropology "Lacan and Lévi-Strauss in 1956" in the review *Figures de la Psychanalyse*.

The translator, Marc du Ry, is a psychoanalyst working in London and a member of CFAR. He also runs academiclanguages.com.

To a few others

Introduction

Freud gave up the therapeutic benefits of hypnotic suggestion; he also limited the tools of the treatment to a speech invited to speak of what it did not know it knew. From that point on he came up against the facts of resistance, amnesia, and transference. To account for them, he constructed some theories which scandalized the way we think: the theories of repression, of the unconscious, of libido and of the death drive. Can one learn these, and if so how? Can one learn to make one's neurosis intelligible to someone else and spark their desire to separate from their symptoms . . . and if so how?

Applied to psychic suffering, psychoanalysis has a rather paradoxical relation to therapeutics: it has to suspend the therapeutic aim and encourage, by means of the transference neurosis, the development of a new form of neurosis. It is driven less by the desire to cure, console, or pardon than a desire to know and a desire for difference.

It is within the field of science, yet it has a curious relation to science: by insisting on the truth of what is said in the symptom, it recognizes the incidence of sexuality in the psyche, there where modern science has defined itself by banishing the truth of sexuality from the field of knowledge. In its theorizing, it has the singular duty of acknowledging the specific nature of not-knowing at work in the passion for ignorance, and has to force the limits one encounters when trying to think the impossible at play in a sexuality marked by language. How can one formulate the appropriate training needed to accede to this discipline of thought and this praxis, a training which, since 1926, has been the subject of debates and splits in the psychoanalytic movement?

Surprise and some suspicion have given me the encouragement to hazard this enquiry into the training of the psychoanalyst; but if this was enough to deal the cards of our questions it was not enough to master the game. As in an analysis, it is the master signifiers of a story I was unaware of that have dictated my reading and led me to shed some received ideas.

We were very surprised that a single saying of Lacan's from 1973 could become dogma to such an extent that it rendered the question of training superfluous for many of his students. During a study day of the Freudian School of Paris, Lacan said, "I never said anything about psychoanalytic training [formation].[1] I only spoke of formations of the unconscious". He did not say, "I never spoke of the training of the analyst", as the saying is often quoted, for he knew well that he had spoken of it, often, to the point of saying his teaching was devoted to it. But it is true that he never spoke of "psychoanalytic training", which evokes a professional training. This same intervention should nevertheless alert us to his paradoxical handling of chosen terms. After having said he tried to get rid of the term "didactic", he specified that an analysis is "didactic" when the subject discovers the articulated knowledge of which he is an effect. Just as he kept the use of this term for a long time, he liberally employed the term "training" [formation], whether in the sense of the action of forming (a concept, the ego, the superego, a delusion, a symptom, a complex, a psychoanalyst) or of its result (moral, mental, delusions, or familial formations, formations of the mind, the I, the unconscious, the ego as formation, and the psychoanalyst as formation). The French language allowed him to play with the ambiguity of a word at the heart of traditional grammar as in the expression "word formation". Doubtless the connotations of "training" (whether in dressage, horticulture, or artillery) could not provide similar resonances. With *Bildung*, other associations come into play, which we will evoke later. I was surprised, then, at the neglect of this term in favour of that of "transmission".

This doxa underlying the mistaken quotation includes the idea that Lacan broke with the system of training current in the IPA, which he criticized, and that he defined the treatment as the sole place of training, leaving the reference to the institution as uncertain, indeed unnecessary. It is true that the identification of the IPA with its system of training is central, both in reality and in Lacan's satirical rendition in 1956.

Moreover, as people tend to think that Freud wanted the analytic institution the way it turned out, they quickly conclude that Freud wanted the kind of training organized by the IPA, and that Lacan made a major break with this. It is this opinion that aroused my suspicion. I preferred to let myself be guided by the recurrent references of Lacan to Freud's thoughts in 1926 in order to form the hypothesis that his return to Freud included questions of training, and that Freud took a more subtle position than that ascribed to him regarding institutionalized training.

There was a tension between this hypothesis and the notion of a break operated by Lacan, especially in the "Proposition of 1967 on the psychoanalyst of the School". The work of two pupils of Lacan on the question of training, an article in *Scilicet* in 1976, "On the history of the training of analysts", and the book by Moustapha Safouan of 1983, *Jacques Lacan and the Question of the Training of Analysts*, were constructed, in their very architecture, on the supposed gap between a training "before Lacan" and the training "with Lacan", guaranteed by the proposition that instituted the *pass*. I have tried to close this gap, map it, and situate it in its true time and place.

With this surprise, suspicion, and aforementioned hypothesis, I have walked a line between history (legend, fable, *Historie*) as told, which I have read and listened to, and history (*Geschichte*) as a historian would write it and which I have not actually done. By allowing the play of complementarity between history and structure, I have taken the risk of making a construction. I wished to construct training as a question, in that place "between science and fiction" in which Michel de Certeau placed psychoanalysis and history, that place which Freud assigned to the psychoanalyst so that he might construct there the truth of a beginning that was necessarily lost.

Note

1. Translator: to clarify some plays on words in the original I have used square brackets. The French "formation" has almost always been translated as "training", in order to make the arguments clearer in their bearing on the question of psychoanalytic training. This has meant at times losing some of the resonances of the word "formation", but hopefully the reader will bear this in mind, especially given the "professional" connotation of the term "training" which the author discusses and questions in the text.

CHAPTER ONE

The First Analysts

A testimony

During the Weimar congress of the Internationale Psychoanalytische Vereinigung (IPV), a woman told Freud of her desire to learn psychoanalysis. Freud laughed a lot at the ardour of Lou Andreas-Salomé. A year later, in 1912, after six months of "self-taught preparatory studies", he allowed her to take part in the Wednesday evening meetings. He wrote to her in October 1912: "we shall all endeavour to make available to you the little there is in psychoanalysis that can be demonstrated and shared" (Andreas-Salomé, 1965, p. 31). During the winter semesters she followed Freud's lectures and Tausk's courses, whom she found too servile in his Freudianism, and she took part in the Wednesday discussions of the Vienna Psychoanalytic Society. The Wednesday evening walks and the long Sunday visits at Freud's home wove a web of friendship, affection, and intellectual collaboration lasting twenty-five years. Their correspondence was pursued in "complete and unreserved frankness". From 1913, she participated in the publication of *Imago*; in 1917, she asked for guidance in the analysis of a little girl, in which she felt a bit lost. In 1922, in Gottingen, and in Koenigsberg in 1923–1924, she conducted a few training analyses of doctors. It is only in 1922 that, thanks to a lacuna in the statutes, she became a full member of the Vienna Psychoanalytic Society, where she always felt most fully at home. Anna Freud, the "girl-Anna", delivered the joint paper for their formal admission.

Lou Andreas-Salomé would never forget the "serious", even lugubrious, tone with which Freud warned his listeners of the difficulties of psychoanalysis, pointing to the resistance an alert and conscious person would, almost of necessity, bring to it because this resistance belonged normally and not pathologically to the psyche. She saw in this "a deliberate attempt to scare us away" (Andreas-Salomé, 1965, p. 32). How could one not, in fact, be afraid of a discovery that could only have been made in the pathological domain, "there where inner life renounces something of itself through its failings" (*ibid.*, p. 17)? She remembered, when she heard Freud for the first time, that this was the thought that took hold of her as she encountered "the Freudian thing" for the very first time while reading Swoboda. An interest she characterized as "neutral and objective" (*ibid.*, p. 18) had been awakened by "the lure of a path opening new sources" (*ibid.*, p. 19).

This was the first reason she gave when Freud spoke to her of the way she came into analysis, giving herself over to it so deeply. From what she related of the talk, it is not clear how the major encounters of her past could have formed this interest in a knowledge which had its source in the experience of certain personal difficulties. It is clear that her meetings with Paul Rée, Nietschze, and Rilke, as well as her intimate attraction to Spinoza, her interest in theology, philology, and poetry, predisposed her to receive psychoanalysis as a "gift". Freud is amused by this third reason: "I really think you look on analysis as a sort of Christmas present" (*ibid.*, p. 90); even though it is but the consequence, however decisive, of the encounter with a "science in progress" which "always allows a return to beginnings" (*ibid.*, p. 90). It is this beginning which is at the start of analysing (*Psychanalysieren*): in Freud's own analysis, there was accomplished "in the very act of the mind" what appears to us afterwards as a human condition for becoming "ourselves" in the simplest sense (Pfeiffer, 1966, pp. 56–57). This encounter affected her: analysis became not only a choice of profession to her but "that by which my life always guides itself".

Both her diary, "In Freud's school" (Andreas-Salomé, 1965), and her correspondence testify to the way she fulfilled her desire to devote herself to analysis; they testify to the way her encounter with Freud and his companions made her initial desire an informed desire; they show what an analytic training could be before it became institutionalized.

At her first Wednesday evening meeting, Lou Andreas-Salomé could not but notice the gap between what Freud wrote and what he had just said. His answer to her explains his position: "my *last* formulation". She thus discovered that his "theory was never rigidly fixed but was based on his changing experience". This model of a researcher steadfastly advancing, without respite, constituted Freud's greatness for her and gave a particular meaning to the dogmatism imputed to him: it was simply a way of putting milestones on the paths of this research which advanced to new frontiers, reserved the right to impose concepts born from difficulties (like the "drive") and "turned problems of psychic life into steps forward for science".

It is to this position of researcher, and not to some paternal complex, that she attributed the complexity of some of Freud's traits: a nostalgic desire for the solitude of the time before the analytic school and the public he nonetheless wanted; an egoism which poorly tolerated an independent and aggressive mind at its side while wishing for a freedom without dogmatic restraints for his disciples. This complexity was sorely tried during the times of the splits in the analytic movement. In 1912, it was already ten years since Freud had began to work with a few others, on the development of analysis, its transmission, treatments, and training the first analysts. The price paid for these new steps was the loss of Wilhelm Fliess's friendship. By making analysis exist, by making it "ex-sist" to him and to Fliess, who shared his discovery, he lost the friendship of the man who was an active witness of the formation of his own desire as analyst. Fliess was his first audience and addressee of a supposed knowledge. 1912 was the year of the first separations, which were to have a definite influence on the training of Lou Andreas-Salomé.

Despite the definitive break between Freud and Alfred Adler, Andreas-Salomé met with the latter and participated in some of his evening seminars, while respecting the split Freud asked her to maintain. She had bitter disputes with the man who, for her, remained but a psychology pupil of Marx and initiated her own split with him. Her bent for synthesis, no doubt strengthened by her previous training, philosophical above all, could have led her to system builders like Jung and Adler. Freud often emphasized her way of thinking, so different from his own, and from which he did not fail to draw benefit by letting her commentaries work on him, her way of "adjusting and completing fragments until a construction is produced", where he would stick with the fragmentary and with discontinuity. He clearly identified how he won her confidence:

> by the way of the ego-libido you have observed how I work, step by step, without the inner need for completion, continually under the pressure of the problem immediately on hand and taking infinite pains not to be diverted from the path. [*ibid.*, p. 61]

As both a witness to and as agent of the concept of narcissistic libido, Lou Andreas-Salomé could assess the theoretical and practical, as well as personal, issues at stake in these splits, which Freud abhorred but was resigned to. When he asked her to take on the role of "third party" to judge his "On the history of the psychoanalytic movement" (Freud, 1914d), she tried to explain the process that turns a misunderstanding into a split. For purely personal reasons, a new point of departure is substituted for the theoretical core. Yet she believed this to be a necessary displacement: "All true revolutions are subject to abuse, but from its very nature Freudian psychoanalysis calls forth this abuse in a completely new fashion" (Andreas-Salomé, 1965, p. 17). In a decisive way, in fact; in analysis "we only know what we experience" and resistance is, for all of us, at the heart of our experience. Analysis progresses *with* this resistance, and the resistance to doctrine is just one form this can take. "Accusing, denouncing and unmasking" (*ibid.*, p. 19) were the tasks repugnant to Freud, yet necessary to analysis.

She used the imagery of core and periphery, of tree, graft, and reject to articulate and guide herself in her disagreement with Freud on certain points. Each person's small kernel of subjectivity can profit from the margins around Freud's work, margins he himself would not refuse to question, but "what belongs to analysis must remain intact". Her constant worry not to misinterpret what belongs to the core of analysis earned her a friendly compliment from Freud: "you were born to understand" (*eine Versteherin par excellence*), to which he added that his way of darkening things on purpose to concentrate on an obscure point did not render him so mole-like as not to rejoice in the feedback she sent back to him. One could speculate that he was not immune to the objections she would formulate in 1931 concerning religion and artistic creation. Did they touch the kernel or the periphery?

If the specific scientific project of analysis is to let theory be shaped by experience, because, more than in other sciences of the mind, here we only know what we experience, its conflicts will be more difficult to appease and its struggles more bitter than anywhere else. This is because the misunderstandings at work in splits are an almost inevitable effect of the intertwining of theory and subjectivity, experience and knowledge. The "Wednesday round table", the "kind of fraternity" to which analysis had introduced her were, for Lou Andreas-Salomé, the very example of an "honest community" (*ehrlichen Gemeinschaft*) in which the probity of each in relation to himself guaranteed loyalty between "brothers" in battle. But was the transformation of a theoretical kernel into "absolute dogma" enough to substitute for the presence of Freud, who guaranteed both cohesion and the space needed for battle?

Lou Andreas-Salomé believed in the necessity of turning this theoretical kernel into "absolute dogma" so that it could attract a wider range of followers. She was very happy, in 1917, that the *Introductory Lectures on Psychoanalysis* (Freud, 1915–1917) gave a shape to the very personal construction of Freud, so that its meaning and value could be appreciated by outsiders, "lay" people like herself.

Better than anyone, even Freud—to whom she addressed the truth of her complaint in the form of a productivity which was too intermittent, uncertain, and subject to mood and health—she articulated the way the object of analysis only allowed itself to be approached in these discontinuous ways. "For however scientific the method of investigation is, the Unconscious will always tend to elude it, as dreams elude us on waking. It will always require an almost unnatural exertion to dedicate oneself to this subject" (Andreas-Salomé, 1965, p. 52). She added, perhaps following Freud's advice, that this effort might only be possible "by keeping up the habit of self-analysis and especially the analysis of one's patients" (*ibid.*). In the very intermittence of theoretical production, the object of analysis gives the "seal of its authenticity".

Now that the masses besiege the edifice and seek to obtain authorization to enter, what form of "honest community" can house such a strange rapport with knowledge and with the very foundations of analysis, as well as the equally necessary attempt to transmit this particular knotting of knowledge and experience? Lou Andreas-Salomé does not tell us. This woman, to whom Freud addressed himself as impartial judge and who, like a child whose dream is fulfilled by a present, signed the letter of acceptance into the Vienna Society with pride and humour as "member-Lou", kept a very singular position with respect to this cause-thing (*Sache*) to which she devoted a third of her life. She did not participate in the "business" in the same way as the "six elder brothers", according to the repeated error of Freud. He was not worried in Lou's case that, as he put it in a letter to Ernest Jones dated 18 November 1920, "business is devouring science" (Paskaukas, 1993). This risk that business would absorb the time and leisure needed for scientific work was one he took with his brothers, those brothers who were just a little too much like sons for him to include himself in the count, if that was the wish indicated by his error. (The number of brothers wrongly assigned to Lou [six instead of five] represents, in fact, the number of members belonging to the Secret Committee at that time, including Freud.) Yet, he offered her a ring, as he had to those in the Secret Committee, and, in his funerary tribute, he counted her as one of the "battle companions". Something of Freud's division in his struggle to carry the destiny of his invention can be felt here; analysis today inherits this division, and it is situated in an elective way in the question of the training of analysts.

Freud's way

The psychoanalytic institution was still in its infancy when Freud had to deal with the "pathology of associations", of which Ferenczi had warned analysts the moment they were about to organize themselves into the IPV. To the classical pathologies (narcissism, struggles for primacy, filial conflicts with authority) was now added the difficulty Freud's disciples had in sustaining the core notions of the unconscious, repression, and libido. With these concepts, Freud had responded to the facts he encountered (gaps in memory, resistance, and transference) once he had given up on hypnotic suggestion and invented a method of directed speech governed by the rule of free association. This rule, which became fundamental, was precisely the means by which resistance, transference, and the psychic formations related to the unconscious could manifest themselves. The split with Steckel involved subjective givens more than theoretical conflicts; Freud considered that Steckel remained faithful to analysis despite having wronged him. The dissidences of Adler and Jung revealed a resistance to the core notions and a refusal to acknowledge the facts they answered to. It was, for Freud, the moment to specify what should be called analysis and what had better be called by another name. For these facts and these theories, scandalous to thought, constitute the "agreed ground of the premises of analysis", terrain which one could not abandon without leaving analysis. The positions of Adler and Jung illustrate how resistance and transference are at work in relation to the doctrine that seeks to account for them. How can one, from then on, take on board the fact that neurotic investment in theory can be at the root of false paths as well as discoveries? How should one prepare analysts to recognize these facts and sustain theories that generate such an aversion?

Confronted with those he had henceforth to consider as adversaries of analysis, Freud continued to think, in 1914, that one's position in relation to dreams and their interpretation was paramount. In conformity with what his own experience had taught him, he thought, during those years, that the dream, being an *analogon* of the symptom, "as far as a good dreamer and an individual not too far removed from the norm was concerned", the kind of analysis which was his own might suffice. No doubt he did not fully appreciate the fact that the terrifying, anguishing, unnameable image would wake up a normal dreamer while he, Freud, by dint of his "defiant courage in the search for truth" (Letter to Andreas-Salomé, dated 28 July 1929, in Pfeiffer, 1966, p. 182), would pursue the search for truth up to the moment of recognition of what Lacan would call the "acephalic nature of the subject". Yet, Freud knew, since the dream of Irma's injection, that that is where the key to the dream, to neurosis and to the treatment was to be found. The question was how to transmit it. Could one teach it?

In the text of 1904, in which he described his method objectively in the third person, Freud presented the interpretation of dreams as an initiation to the technique which allows one to extract "the pure metal of the repressed thoughts from the ore of the unintentional ideas" (Freud, 1904a, p. 252). Ferenczi confirmed how each new reading of this text (which were numerous by 1908) gave him new knowledge and fresh insights (Falzeder & Brabant, 1996, 66 Fer[1]). Then Freud specified in 1912 that handling the interpretation of dreams was not an art in itself: "it has to answer to the totality of the treatment". Between these two dates, his own experience and those of the first analysts had permitted the drawing of the outlines as well as the pitfalls, both unexpected and foreseen, inherent to this method. In his letters, as well as during their meetings, Freud often and gladly offered as a gift to his companions this "hardest of conquests"—technique—but to respond as "an old hand" to the requests for advice from Karl Abraham, Sandor Ferenczi and Ernest Jones was not enough, and neither was his lecture at the College of Physicians in 1904. He became aware of the gap between his way of practising the "rules" taught him by his practice "at his own expense by using other methods", and the attitude of his pupils. He had never felt fear at remaining at a loss with a patient, as Abraham had, too anxious to triumph rapidly over the symptom; his indifference towards his patients never led him to "be inclined to consider their affairs as his own", as happened to Ferenczi. His exchanges of 1908 that dealt with the major technical questions of handling time, transference, and what he would call, a year later, countertransference, led him to plan to write " a general method of analysis". Ferenczi was unabashedly delighted, without a hint of the rivalry which marked Abraham. He gauged the extent to which "there must, however, be something painful in simply yielding this knowledge, with such difficulty and so many sacrifices, to us youngsters." (Falzeder & Brabant, 1996, Fer 23). But doubtless Freud could only spare his followers from "part of the grind and—part of the cost" (Falzeder, 2002, p. 25).

Freud never published this methodology, giving up on it in 1910, just as he gave up on *metapsychology*; instead, he opted for the piecemeal, publishing six decisive articles, on the technique of the treatment between 1912 and 1915. First published in the *Zentralblatt für Psychoanalyse* and then in the *Zeitschrifft für Psychoanalyse*, they were ultimately published together in 1918 in the collectionj of writings on the theory of neuroses (Freud, 1911e, 1912b, 1912e, 1913c, 1914g, 1915a). In 1912, Freud announced that, besides articles bringing new developments in psychoanalysis, the *Zentralblatt* proposed to present work of "didactic nature and technical content", setting out clearly what was already acquired for whoever is learning and aiming to give to the beginner appropriate indications which might save him time and effort. In 1914 he wrote about his restraint and his choice:

> I myself did not venture to put forward a still unfinished technique and a theory still in the making with an authority which would probably have enabled the others to avoid some wrong turnings and ultimate disasters. [Freud, 1914d, p. 26]

He claimed to have preferred the autonomy of intellectual workers, with their swift independence from a master. He recognized it was a difficult, even risky, choice if not supported by "long and secure discipline".

This discipline, which goes against the master–pupil relationship of a training, was that of analysis and its fundamental rule. Already, at the Nuremberg Congress of 1910, Freud posited its necessity: ". . . No analyst goes further than his own complexes and internal resistances permit" (1910d, p. 145). It is, therefore, fitting to require of an analyst that

> he shall begin his activity with a self-analysis (*Selbstanalyse*) and continually carry it deeper while he is making his observations on his patients. Anyone who fails to produce results in a self-analysis of this kind may at once give up any idea of being able to treat patients by analysis. [*ibid.*, p. 145]

Two years later, in June 1912, he took a further step in his "Recommendations to physicians practising psychoanalysis". He no longer said that one became an analyst through the analysis of one's own dreams, but paid homage to the Zurich school for having beefed up the requirement that anyone wishing to practise should first submit to analysis with a qualified analyst. While telling one's thoughts to a stranger "without being driven to it by illness" is certainly a sacrifice, it is also a gain of time and an economy of affect, allowing the possibility of gaining access to a conviction concerning one's own person and body which no lecture or book can give. He who neglects to have himself analysed exposes to risk not only his patients, but himself, as well as analysis, for the temptation will be great to "project outwards some of the peculiarities of his own personality, which he has dimly perceived, into the field of science, as a theory having universal validity" (Freud, 1912e, pp. 116–117).

It was with the notion of a specific training analysis, even though no such term existed in the text, contrary to what the French translation would have us believe, that the premises of the questions that recur in the history of analytic training were given: a distinction between therapeutic and training analyses, correlated with the supposed normality of the analysands, the end required for the analysis of an analyst, and "the durable psychic relation" established between the new analyst and his "proposer" (*Einführenden*).

It is important to note that Freud did not make a rule out of this requirement and that he did not always go as far as Ferenczi's radical reading of it. At this date of June 1912, most of the inner circle had not yet started an analysis with another analyst. On 30 July 1912, Jones told Freud of Ferenczi's wish that Freud systematically analyse all future analysts. This small group of men could

> represent the pure theory, unadulterated by personal complexes, and thus build an unofficial inner circle in the *Verein* and serve as centres where others (beginners) could come and learn the work. If that were only possible it would be an ideal solution. [Paskaukas, 1993, letter 80]

Freud turned a deaf ear. The combination of his "taste for the Romanesque" and Jones' romantic imagination transformed Ferenczi's proposition into a project for a Secret Committee, whose "puerile" character, recognized by Freud, reminds us of the secret writings he shared as an adolescent with Silberstein. Jones' dream of "the small unified group, destined, like Charlemagne's knights, to guard the empire and be their master's police" would certainly have the task of "purging, as far as possible, the theory of any excrescences and of coordinating our unconscious goals with the requirements and interests of the movement". Its members would be named by Freud, but not all, nor would all be systematically analysed by him. His silence in the correspondence makes it difficult to analyse his non-response to Ferenczi's proposition: deafness? Deliberate refusal? Repression? In the Committee, he deliberately won a margin of freedom by instituting a division: "I will give free rein to my fantasy, and probably leave the role of Censorship to you". At the right moment, he certainly made use of this freedom by opposing the very censors he had instituted.

The homage Freud paid to the Zurich school in abandoning the model of self-analysis has a bitter taste when one remembers that not long after this Jung would denounce Freud's own self-analysis with brutal insolence. Freud had to swallow the shame this letter caused him when he told Rank, Sachs, and Ferenczi of the painful event: "My construction of the totemic feast proves itself in practice; from all sides, the brothers fall upon me, first among them, of course, the 'founders of religion'" (Falzeder & Brabant, 1996, 359 F). Ferenczi had subtly analysed how this rebellion against Freud's authority expressed Jung's desire to except himself from the very "analytic community" of pupils he had always favoured. According to him, Jung could not bear the fact that the pupils, like himself, were treated as patients; in doing this, he denied what he asked for and opted instead for a "fraternal Christian community" coherent with the position of "saviour" he held in the treatment (*ibid.*, 362 F).

The master–pupil relationship enshrines an inequality in the relation to knowledge. When Freud, in his lectures, mixed the positions of pupil and patient, in effect he substituted for this inequality the dissymmetry at work in the transference. He warned his listeners of the dangers analysis brings with it and which necessarily compromise its teaching: "Do not be annoyed, then, if I begin by treating you in the same way as these neurotic patients" (Freud, 1915–1917, p. 15). Adapting oneself to the discipline of analysis in every aspect of work was a consequence of this, and Freud tried to maintain it in the Wednesday meetings. Thus, up to 1908, everyone present was obliged to speak. In 1912, still, Freud started the meetings by reminding them that "we ought to speak without shame or holding back anything about the subjects we study, however shocking" (Andreas-Salomé, 1991). It is by submitting to the fundamental rule that the analyst is formed, in his treatment as much as in his relation to theory and his practice, and thus to the working community that can only be called analytic on this condition. Freud insisted on this with the authority given by the inaugural act of *psychoanalysing*. But the question was how to maintain this orientation when the extension of knowledge and the growing number of practitioners multiplied the "needs of training". Did the way chosen by Freud in 1910 with the International Association and repeated in 1912 with the Secret Committee, of organizing a vigilant transmission within a centralized and policed movement, answer to the specific constraints of this transmission?

What other imaginary and theory of the collective would have been needed to allow Ferenczi's idea of founding the extension and transmission of analysis on the exhaustive analyses of the analysts? It would have required a radical distinction between the power of mastery and the authority at play in the dissymmetry of the analytic relation to contribute to the founding of an analytic community which did not turn into the "fraternal Christian community" of Jung. The model that prevailed had the form and power of those organized masses of which Freud, in 1912, had not yet written the theory; Freud left it to his battle companions to take the initiative in modelling the training of analysts along these lines, while reserving the right not to apply this model himself and even to go against it. In the years preceding this operation, as in the years that followed, writings and journals remained his major and constant worry as a means to support his "problem child". They were an important tool in both his own and his pupils' training.

Budapest

"My problem child" is how Freud described psychoanalysis in a letter to Ferenczi after the Budapest Congress, speaking of his satisfaction in seeing his life's work protected (Falzeder & Brabant, 1996, 759F). It is indeed in that city that the organization for the training of analysts was sketched out, before becoming the official model in Berlin. The years 1918–1920 were decisive in this and evince the impact the First World War and its political aftermath had on the destiny of analysis.

With its many privations, the abandoning of meetings and correspondence, the mobilization of analysts, and the suspension of activity of local groups, these war years were a sore trial for the analytic movement and for most analysts on the continent. In July 1915, Freud asked himself when the scattered members of their "apolitical community" could meet again and whether politics would not have corrupted them meanwhile (Pfeiffer, 1966, p. 33); right from the start of the war he let Jones know "that it has been decided between them not to consider each other as enemies" (letter 205). During the isolation of the war, in this time during which "one has vigorously to remind oneself that there are still a few people for whom it is worth writing" (Falzeder, 2002, p. 342), Freud continued the task of developing and transmitting analysis. He kept both *Imago* and the *Zeitschrift* going, gave lectures during the winters of 1916 and 1917, and worked on the project of "Preliminary essays on metapsychology". Whereas the lectures embody a stable body of convictions strengthened by twenty-five years of experience, the title "metapsychology" already indicates its exploratory nature; seven of them would be destined "for suppression and silence". Together with the 1915 "Thoughts for the Times on War and Death", these two endeavours counter the brutality and lies promoted by war, the confusion with which it had struck the most lucid minds, and—supreme disillusionment—the enlisting of science it operated. And yet, this very war would unexpectedly provide official recognition for psychoanalysis, something not without paradoxical effects on the theoretical advances of Freud in these same years.

Despite some diffidence, a number of doctors in Berlin, London, and Budapest who were busying themselves with war neuroses were forced to recognize some of the factors that analysis had isolated in peacetime neuroses, whether traumatic or not; the success obtained in their treatment by means of the cathartic method encouraged some rapprochement with analysis. But this rapprochement would encounter a doctrinal difficulty of analysis, which would be reinforced by the classic resistance to sexual aetiology. Was "an impartial attitude and a little good will" going to overcome this difficulty (Freud, 1919d, p. 208)? The case of Ernst Simmel is interesting on this point. The honesty of his defence of psychoanalysis was not enough to overcome his strong resistance, noted by Abraham, to the sexual factor, the "red rag" of sexuality (Pfeiffer, 1966, p. 83). Freud was confident: "I think a year of training would make a good analyst of him. His behaviour is correct" (Falzeder, 2002, p. 372). Simmel started his analysis with Abraham, and two years later would become co-founder of the Berlin Institute with Max Eitingon. It is important to note that Freud knew how to understand the way Simmel's resistance met with a point of non-knowing in theory. The application of libido theory outside of transference neuroses remains, in fact, a problem; it already necessitated the notion of narcissistic libido; it requires a further exploration of the relations between anxiety, fright, and narcissistic libido. The specific question of war neuroses led Freud to the notion of "internal enemy" and "elementary traumatic neurosis". What was broached here and necessitated by this point of not-knowing was nothing less than the theoretical reworking of *Beyond the Pleasure Principle*.

Freud's theoretical rigour, his ability to confront the stumbling blocks of doctrine, was not scuppered by his concern, just as real, for the recognition and extension of psychoanalysis. The Budapest Conference, held at the end of September 1918 in the presence of government officials from Germany, Austria, and Hungary, constituted the public moment of this recognition and gave hope of interest in analysis from public health services. Abraham, Ferenczi, and Simmel presented their ideas on the analysis of war neuroses (Internationale Zeitschrift für Psychoanalyse, IPV, Vienna, 1920, pp. 52–57; Zur Psychoanalyse der Kriegsneurosen, IPV, Leipzig and Vienna, 1919). Freud himself laid more stress on social factors than before and this was going to have more of an impact on the coming organization of training than his theoretical handling of the themes of death, masochism, trauma, "internal enemy", and ego conflict, which were just round the corner. In 1910, at the first IPV congress, Freud had already made some utopian utterances which he straight away qualified by adding that anyone aiming for "an ideal prophylactic for neurotic illness" should avoid the attitude of "a fanatic for hygiene or therapy". Yet, he maintained that the practice of analysis was not solely therapeutic nor scientific but contributed to "enlightening the masses" (*Aufklärung*). This enlightening and the social influence to be expected from it, promised to resolve the enigma of neurosis by calling it by its "secret name". It would be the "general effect" of the resolution of neurosis on the social (Freud, 1910d, pp. 148–151). The social accent of 1918 was different, even if Freud placed it in a far from utopian future; the hypothesis was now rather therapeutic and numeric. The growth in the number of analysts made possible by "some kind of organisation" would allow for the treatment of "a considerable mass of the population" (Freud, 1919a, p. 167). If, at the same time, the social conscience of the state were to recognize the right of the poor to psychical aid, conditions would be right for setting up institutions for the treatment of a large number of ill people. Free care and recourse to hypnotic influence were part of the baser material Freud did not refrain from mixing with the "pure gold" of analysis, even though only the latter was going to be effective.

These remarks Freud made in Budapest were going to be important for the organization of training put together in Berlin by Eitingon, Abraham, and Simmel. But, before entering into the logic of this organization, which isolated elements from the whole field of analysis not separated before, it is important to look at the short period in which Budapest became the "homeland of analysis" (Falzeder & Brabant, 1996, Fer 774) and saw the first blueprint of an institute.

When Freud's article "On the teaching of psychoanalysis in universities" was published in Hungarian in Budapest at the end of March 1919, the ephemeral Hungarian Soviet Republic, inspired by the Bolshevik revolution, was already eight days old, and Ferenczi was about to be appointed professor "for psychoanalysis" and director of an analytic clinic (Freud, 1919j). The "somewhat adventurous" politics of Dr Radó, and the support of Gyorgy Lukacs, then education secretary, thus satisfied the two petitions from medical students which had requested university teaching of analysis against very strong opposition (Falzeder & Brabant, 1996, 767 Fer and 814 Fer). In this circumstantial text, Freud showed the same reticence he expressed to Ferenczi in private, and defined the analyst's point of view in a few lines: the fact that analysis is excluded from the university has produced an organization in which analysis can do without the university. Publications, meetings of associations, personal contact with older and more experienced analysts, one's own treatment, treatment under supervision from a recognised analyst, all suffice "in a perfectly satisfactory manner" to give someone the theoretical indications and practical experience of analysis. We find again here the tenor of statements Freud made in 1916 "before an audience of doctors and laymen of both sexes" (Freud, 1915–1917, p. 9): analysis is known only by "hearsay", second-hand; one only verifies the truth of what is said by one's own personal analytic experience (*am eigenen Leib*) and by the study of one's own personality; on this occasion one can pick up from one's analyst the more subtle technique of the procedure (*ibid.*, p. 19). To describe this singular and specific way of learning analysis and its practice, which involves neither demonstration nor proof, Freud never uses the term "training" (*Ausbildung*). On the other hand, he did use it for doctors and scientists.

That the university should recognize the importance of analysis for the training of doctors was another question that the article addressed. It was a chance for Freud to emphasise again that the teaching of analysis leaves but little margin for presentation and experimentation, and, in his reference to "the fertilizing effect" of analytic thought on other disciplines, to assign to analytic method some ambition in the field of knowledge. (The sentence added by Ferenczi "for tactical reasons" [Falzeder & Brabant, 1996, 803 Fer] shifts the emphasis of the article: he calls for the addition of a psychiatric section for a "psychoanalytical practice of psychiatry".) Because it is applicable not only to the functioning of psychical pathology, but also to questions posed by art, philosophy, and religion, the "fecundation" of those branches of science such as history of literature, mythology, history of religions and civilizations, "would certainly contribute greatly towards forging a closer link, in the sense of a *universitas literarum*, between medical science and the branches of learning which lie within the sphere of philosophy and the arts" (Freud, 1919a, p. 173). The ambition of this proposition, seemingly archaic in its reference to a medieval university grouping of arts and sciences, was nothing less than bringing together again—differently—what scientific and academic modernity had separated.

In the period between the declaration of 1918 and the article of 1919, Freud had witnessed the way the fortunes of Hungarian politics affected the destiny of analysis in that country. It explains the difference between his two statements; the social accent of the conference shifts: "We are not made for any form of official existence, we need our complete independence . . . may God protect us from our friends" (Falzeder & Brabant, 1996, 808 Fer). Yet, it was in Budapest that the first project for a centre of treatment and training was both born and abandoned, a project associated with the name of Anton von Freund.

The trajectory of this doctor in philosophy and rich brewer from Budapest, patient and friend of Freud, brought into the Secret Committee by him, was a significant counterpoint to the training to be created in Berlin. It was not without prudence that Freud, aware of the neurotic character of Freund's compulsion to give and help, accepted in 1918 the setting up of a trust, managed by the mayor of Budapest and in part available to him, to promote the general interests of analysis. Here, Freud's choices were clear: "At the forefront of our projects . . . there is publishing and the creation of two prizes; any other projects I deem less important". Covering the publishing expenses would remain his main concern when negotiating the funds of the endowment.

The brief passage of von Freund through the history of the analytic movement is not only a question of patronage, however. He consulted Freud, who had already analysed his wife, in a moment of post-operative psychosis. As the delusioned idea receded to bring out the hysterical neurosis, "a good and proper analysis began" which, Freud noted a bit later, "as it has the aim of reordering a human being . . . can be pursued beyond the disappearance of symptoms". This necessitated dismantling "bits of his primordial savagery" and gave Freud occasion to note the gap between the analytic clinic and official psychiatry (Falzeder & Brabant, 1996, 733 F, 735 F, 753 F, 780 F, 787 F, 801 F, 814 Fer, 815 Fer). During this analysis, which left him, according to Freud, "healed from his incursion into psychosis in the form of a half-analysed neurosis", a new desire decided itself for von Freund, no longer to help analysis but to practise it, which he did on his return to Budapest, rejoicing in the discoveries he made each day with a hysteric patient. A few months later, in the autumn of 1919, facing death, he decided to leave a major part of his trust to an institute for treatment and training. His death undid the project at the moment of its conclusion (Falzeder & Brabant, 1996, letters 826 Fer, 827 F).

The correspondence of Freud with Ferenzci, Abraham, and Jones, the circular letter of Freud to the Secret Committee in

November 1918, and Ferenczi's letter to Eitingon for his admission into the Committee (Wittenberg & Tögel, 1913–1920, pp. 43–46), make clear that the two projects for an institution in Budapest and Berlin do not stem from the initiative of Freud or the Committee, but are singular ones. If the "Centre for scientific training in psychoanalysis" of Budapest had seen the light of day, it would have been run by A. Von Freund, a lay man practising analysis following an analysis begun in a psychotic moment, and would have had Ferenczi as scientific director, a man well aware of the pathology, both familial and narcissistic, of associations. (During the Nuremberg Congress in 1910, most of Ferenzci's speech makes this pathology explicit at the very moment he is proposing the constitution of the International Association (Ferenczi, 1968, Volume I, pp. 166–167).) One can speculate that this would have had some consequence.

Note

1. Here, I use the system of numbering letters from Hoffer's translation of *The Correspondence of Sigmund Freud and Sandor Ferenczi*, edited by Falzeder and Brabant, 1996.

CHAPTER TWO

The Berlin Model

The utopia of therapy for the masses

The moment that the white terror began in August 1919, anti-semitic persecution was unleashed in Hungary. From the autumn of that year, von Freund's condition left no hope. On 18 December 1919, Freud wrote to Ferenczi that they had to give up the project of setting up a treatment and training centre in Budapest, while saving what could be saved by rejecting any form of collaboration with the authorities. The political reversal, which he found traumatic, led Ferenczi to the brink of exile in February 1920 and prompted Melanie Klein, Sandor Radó, Franz Alexander, and Alice and Michael Balint to leave for Berlin. It was in Berlin, on 14 February 1920, that the Polyclinic and Institute were launched, brought to fruition by Eitington and Simmel during the autumn with Abraham's blessing, and it was Berlin which thus became, after Vienna, the active centre where analysis found a new framework for its extension.

It was also in Berlin that the analytic training model was established: the 1930 report on "Ten years of the Berlin Psychoanalytic Training Institute" (*Zehn Jahre Berliner psychoanalytisches Institut*,

1930) has the ring of pioneering enthusiasm. It was an enthusiasm that did not shrink from financial sacrifice. The volunteering of members of the German Psychoanalytic Society and the underpayment of the analysts symbolically balanced Eitingon's investment and thus reduced that portion of *jouissance* which was also invested in it. It was a therapeutic (and social) enthusiasm, legislative (and controlling), didactic (and systematic). Number and extension were the master signifiers; Eitingon's 1922, 1925, and 1928 reports tally with the 1930 dossier (Eitingon, 1923, 1926). Eitingon relates how the long conversations with "his work colleague", the socialist doctor Simmel, gave them the courage to "answer to great needs with so little means". Responding with psychoanalysis to the *Zeitgeist*, which demanded "psychotherapy vociferously", allowed them to turn a "moment of general collapse" into "a favourable opportunity" for analysis. Because of the war, the drafting of analysts into armed service, and their ability to treat war neuroses, psychoanalysis acquired the authority Freud deemed necessary for its development. But to "allow access to analysis of the greatest number of people possible", to thus take literally Freud's utopian wish of 1918 in Budapest, to want to respond to the growth of neurotic distress, were just so many goals which led the practice of analysis into a new thicket of problems of time and number. How could one respond to hundreds of appeals (1955 registered consultations from the founding of the Polyclinic to 1 January 1930) with a small number of analysts?

The solution envisaged was to modify technique from a temporal perspective: reducing the length of the session would increase the number of patients being seen. But this intention was never realized. Eitingon gave two reasons not to go down this route: a half-hour session would require too much discipline from a neurotic, and the time of the session, which he called "real time", ought to be long, "continuous and without respite" in order to "combat the timelessness of the unconscious" (Eitingon, 1923). These reasons were not, however, invoked in relation to the other reduction in time, introduced with the idea of "fractioned analysis". This was the interruption of the analysis by the analyst when he judged the patient to be fit and ready for life.

In the background, one can already detect the issue of standard length sessions as well as the recurrent question of the length of an analysis. Freud had always emphasized that he did not hesitate to modify his technique and that these changes sometimes allowed for decisive facts to be recognized. This was the case when giving up hypnosis for free association, for example, as well as for leaving the subject free to talk about anything rather than centring him on the symptom. Likewise, the recognition of a fact could bring about a change in technique: acknowledging transference, for example, would subordinate the question of dream interpretation. New knowledge, a greater complexity in work, and slowing down the treatment were the results of both of these changes, despite the wish of both analyst and patient to speed things up.

The technical rules Freud transmitted to his circle were taught "from [his] own experience" through long practice (Freud, 1912e, p. 111). If this technique was "the only one suited to [his] individuality", he did not dispute that another doctor, "quite differently constituted", might adopt a different position. In 1924, during the split with Rank, he admitted that a new theoretical discovery might modify technique. There again, to come back to the image of core and periphery, taking into account the unconscious, libido, and transference remained crucial. Perhaps his utopian statement in Budapest had shifted the question; concluding his remarks on the necessity of exploring the "active" technique promoted by Ferenczi, according to precise rules, he had not shrunk from imagining an alliance of the "pure gold" of analysis with other metals to achieve a therapy for the masses. For the treatment of war neuroses, which had been the occasion for this social project, certain disciples had done exactly that by reintroducing hypnosis. It was this therapeutic aim that became a criterion in 1922 in Eitingon's report when weighing up the technical changes envisaged, although this therapeutic aim was curiously transformed into a "battle" against the timelessness of the unconscious. One cannot but question the coherence of this battle against the unconscious and the putting aside of knowledge as a goal ("our aim is not research"): was this the truth of a standard in the making being articulated here?

The second way of resolving the question of number was to filter the demands and decide which cases would be favourable: out of the 1955 consultations, 721 analyses were started. Otto Fenichel's report on therapeutic activity at the Polyclinic brought to light how much the complexity of the task was increased by the contradiction between the goal of therapy, with its concern for a cure, and the twin goals of teaching and research at the Institute (*Zehn Jahre Berliner psychoanalytisches Institut*, 1930, pp. 57–71). The pupils ended their training as therapists in the Polyclinic. The logic of the teaching led them to be assigned the most classical cases of neuroses possible, yet the concern for research could lead to privileging the opposite kind of case. The attempts at diagnostic classification (thirty-one entries) and the table of degrees of cure shed, in their numerical dryness, an interesting light on this contradiction and its effects on the clinic. While Fenichel's classification highlights, in its departure from Freud's nosography, the prevalence given to symptoms, the criteria for the cure show the gap between the analytic and the therapeutic aims. Fenichel, in effect, distinguished an improvement, due to "successful transference", analytically imperfect, from an analytic cure which would imply not only disappearance of symptoms, but "a character change explicable according to analytic reason". It is a distinction that, in a sense, challenged the therapeutic vision which promoted a "fractioned analysis", interrupted by the analyst on the basis of an amelioration which was not a cure in the analytic sense.

Last, the third solution to the problem of number was, of course, to increase the number of analysts. Foreseeable from the beginning, this reason was at the basis of the foundation of the *Berliner Psychoanalytisches Institut*; it was meant to allow a continuous increase in personnel in the Polyclinic and provide an urgent solution to the burning question for Eitingon of how "to reproduce the analytic species". It was, therefore, a question of how to train analysts by means of a methodical set of lectures and a systematic training that gave them the chance to "learn analysis". The order of necessity which dictated the large-scale training of analysts was therefore therapeutic; it was this order of necessity which gave to the Berlin training one of its specific characteristics: Eitingon conceded that it was an organization "on the Prussian model". This rule-based system tended to define a profession by means of the training giving access to it, rather than by means of the object of its practice.

The regulations

Already, in the spring of 1923 in Berlin, a commission was charged with the task of developing directives for a training so that agreement could be reached on the criteria of admission and the *cursus*. In 1925, Jones suggested to Eitingon that they institute an International Teaching Committee within the IPV; he was determined to apply to the analytic institution the principle that ensured victory for the Allies against the powers siding with Germany: unity of command (Paskaukas, 1993, letter 236). Eitingon, who had replaced von Freund in the Secret Committee, accepted with enthusiasm, and, the same year, proposed to the Bad Hamburg Congress a set of rules for the training cycle he thought very simple: a training analysis was an analysis like any other ("only one technique: the right one"), theoretical training was "relatively straightforward" (well-organized lectures and well-grouped candidates), while supervision brought to training candidates the workshop of analysis and the master artisan the beginner needed (Eitingon, 1926). Initially, in Berlin, an "intensive" theoretical training would precede the training analysis which was "an essential part of his curriculum", followed by supervised practice at the Polyclinic. In a later stage, this training analysis would become the first stage of the training, preceding the theoretical *cursus* and the practical one. It was this latter sequence which was standardized in 1925 and which would be subjected to ever greater regulation.

In November 1952, once freed from his duty of discretion by resigning from the Teaching Commission of the San Francisco Institute, Siegfried Bernfeld interpreted the rage for regulation that had possessed the Berliners as the effect of their ambivalence on hearing of Freud's cancer: by means of their authoritarianism and the coercive selection they exercised, they "punished their students for their own ambivalence" (Bernfeld, 1962). Echoing this lecture, only published in 1962, Safouan in turn interpreted it as an acting out on the part of those closest to Freud and his students and their concern to integrate analysis with the medical profession as an alibi for fraternal delinquency (Safouan, 1983, p. 19). The dates do not confirm the factual basis of the interpretation, the Berlin statutes having already been drafted when Freud's illness was made known; but they do not invalidate its correctness, as Freud regularly brought up the issue of his death in relation to the future of analysis.

Bernfeld gave another reason for this regulatory fever, which was that certain people "exiled from the medical profession" did not let up trying to establish analysis within it. In doing so, they were not only looking for recognition from their medical colleagues, but also seeking to establish a "xenophobic" defence against the "cultural revolution" that had propagated an interest in analysis among youth movements, the educational section of socialist parties, among educators, social workers, and artists. Regulation, which aimed at social recognition for the profession and its integration into the "medical establishment" (Clavreul, 1978), was also a way to combat the epidemic diffusion of analysis, a mode of diffusion that had amused Freud (he "savoured" the anecdote of the endemic hearth of Charlottenburg) but which he also feared, for scientific rather than social reasons.

One area in which regulation ruled supreme was the selection of candidates, which was the responsibility of the Teaching Commission. It was a central focus of the directives Berlin was rewriting in 1929, as it concerned personal aptitude, prior training, and motivation for practice. According to Karen Horney, it took a lot of courage to spell out criteria for personal aptitude, for it meant recognizing the limits of the efficacity of analysis: it cannot "turn any human being whatever into an ideal analyst, or even, simply an averagely effective one" (Horney, 1985). The following were deemed necessary: mature personality, trustworthy character, psychological gifts, and the absence of serious neurotic disorders. Given this, one could naturally ask oneself whether the Commission despaired of training analysis or analysis in general, and it comes as no surprise that the very manner of recognizing these qualities provoked some debate.

What a prior training might look like was only clarified later on. Until 1923, the introductory lectures on therapy and practice given by Eitingon and Simmel were reserved for doctors. In 1922, it seemed evident that, of the twenty-five people who had finished their training analyses, only the nineteen doctors would apply analysis to psychotherapy and that the rest would apply it to other work, education or ethnology. On this condition, non-physicians were indeed admitted to the full *cursus* of the training, including practical work. Drafted after Freud's intervention of 1926 and the debate of 1927 on lay analysis, the "Directives" of 1929 specified the training conditions of non-physicians for analytic practice. In addition to the prior university education, only exceptionally replaceable by a practical profession of value or scientific work, a "scientific aptitude" was needed, not required for doctors, and a complementary university education in the fields of biology, sexology, psychology, pathology, and psychiatry, as well as experience of the doctor–patient relationship.

Specific conditions were also laid down concerning the initial engagement of the non-medical candidate prior to the start of his training. Each candidate, doctor or not, "commits himself to not starting in practice of his own accord and not declaring himself a practising analyst before the completion of the training and the authorisation of the Teaching Commission". Non-physicians, moreover, had to commit themselves to respecting the restrictions fixed by the German Psychoanalytical Society, which reserved to doctors the right to diagnosis as well as the treatment of psychoses and borderline cases. Once these conditions were fulfilled, the training analysis, the theoretical and the practical *cursus*, were the same for both types of candidate.

In such a framework, one of the most important questions, that of who can authorize themselves to hold the position of analyst, could not even be formulated. Instead, an answer was given based on criteria of normality and prior training far removed from what is at stake in the question, and decided on by the institution. (This question was formulated by Lacan and put in context only after a major split.) A remark of Lou Andreas-Salomé can illuminate the logic of the answer. Solicited by Eitingon to conduct training analyses of doctors, she was quick to point out to Freud the impasses of these didactic imperatives: "this analysis seemed to be more imposed by Dr Eitingon than wanted by himself (the patient) for mostly he feels too healthy" (Pfeiffer, 1966, p. 116). A year later, she wrote that of the three doctors, the one most suited for analysis "is not in a position to continue the analysis long enough" (*ibid.*, p. 129).

In order to grasp, beyond individual cases, the contradictions inherent in these required analyses imposed on reputedly normal doctors, it is necessary to examine the split instituted between "didactic" and "therapeutic" through the introduction of the training analysis "as an independent branch of analysis" (Sachs, 1985, p. 136). This split would be hidden by what Jones called the "tricky question": analysis as practised by lay people. Yet, perhaps the split was what determined this tricky question. It went hand in hand with a misrecognition, as much of the specific nature of analysis in its paradoxical relation to therapy and to knowledge as of the specific nature of neurosis in its relation to knowledge. Freud had already broached, when writing on infantile sexual theory and in his study of Leonardo, some of the destinies, including the destiny of neuroses, which followed from the sexual desire to know.

The didactic/therapeutic split: a misunderstanding

The published part of the Freud–Abraham correspondence shows the patent disagreement, or tension at the very least, over these issues. When Abraham, in the autumn of 1907, decided to leave his psychiatric hospital post and practise in Berlin as a specialist in nervous and psychic disorders, he counted on two things: the analytic method and his psychiatric training. During his three years at the Burghölzli Clinic in Zurich (where he was the assistant to Eugen Bleuler, with Jung, from December 1904 to December 1907), he had read Freud's texts and worked on the sexual aspect of the problem of dementia praecox, "the one only a small number want to treat" (Falzeder, 2002, p. 1). At his request, Freud had no problem introducing him to physicians in Berlin, in so far as he was willing to be seen as his disciple and pupil without shame. Abraham agreed, and sought Freud's permission to ask his advice. He never commented on the first piece of advice that Freud, in the light of his experience, gave him: "I hope you will make no attempt whatever to win the favour of your new colleagues . . . but will instead turn directly to the public" (ibid., p. 9). Some months later, he had to insist three times to get Freud's advice, which was cautious, on his project to start a lecture course for doctors on the theory of neuroses and dreams. Despite Freud's advice, Abraham continued to address himself to his colleagues, confronting their opposition, and, in 1908, he informed Freud that only doctors would be part of the Berlin Psychoanalytic Association when it was constituted. Sometimes Freud laughed at Abraham's surprise when an official psychiatrist swallowed analysis "whole". But when things became serious, he became firmer: "Well, I am tremendously pleased that so much is going on in Berlin, and that you too are beginning to be convinced of the impossibility of restricting analysis to *doctors*. Best of all is the installation of Sachs" (ibid., p. 427). Abraham's reply shows the extent of the misunderstanding:

My views about bringing in laymen have not changed. The lectures planned by Sachs deal with non-medical matters, and I have always been in agreement with extending this part of our science to lay circles and have indeed furthered it with my own writings. [*ibid.*, pp. 428–429]

This reply emphasizes how the split, recently entrenched in the new training, between training and therapeutic analyses was tied up with the question of lay analysis. Hans Sachs was put in charge of training analyses, now compulsory for the first time, two years after the Budapest Congress voted against Nunberg's proposition to make it a condition for becoming an analyst. That a non-physician like Sachs was called to Berlin as the first training analyst, named as such, paradoxically confirms the split rather than contesting it, as one might think. A training analysis, as opposed to a therapeutic analysis, pursued for purposes of training by candidates who are not too neurotic, could be handed over to a non-physician. Having conducted a large number of such analyses, Sachs, in the light of his experience, would call this split into question in 1927.

The Berlin Institute admitted lay people to practice analysis, subject to the restrictions ruled in 1929 and within the limits advocated by Jones; this was more than the Dutch and American Institutes were to allow. In all this the tenor emanating from Abraham's first letter persisted: analysis was a psychotherapy and psychotherapy was a medical affair; the aim of a training was to bring doctors the analytical knowledge (analysis, theory and practice) which would allow them to practice. This assumption also operated beyond the confines of the Institute, in "lay" form, in which the clinical psychologist was substituted for the doctor. It is less important to wonder at this than it is to realise to what extent this model represents a misunderstanding of Freud's invention and a misrecognition of the specific nature of analysis. This misunderstanding, which probably partially escaped Freud himself, is for a large part due to the way Freud continued to include analysis within medical practice and addressed himself in his articles indifferently to both doctor and analyst. Yet he emphasised the particularity of the analytic method in relation to any other therapeutic approach, envisaged that it required going beyond therapeutics and recognised as analysts non-physicians without requiring of them a complementary medical training.

His lecture at the College of Physicians in Vienna in 1904 allows us to clarify this misunderstanding (Freud, 1905a, p. 258). There, Freud defended the psychotherapeutic method, not as an invention of analysis, but as "the oldest form of medical therapeutics". The doctor cannot dispense with it because "the patient for his part has no intention of renouncing it"; it is, in fact, he who is in control of the psychic factor, which the doctor could only be if he disposed of a scientific psychotherapeutic method. In some respects, analytic knowledge could bring the doctor this scientific dimension through its development of the psychic factor. The project of teaching (*didaskein*) a doctor this knowledge with a view to a reasoned and controlled use of psychotherapy would be grounded in this.

In addressing himself as therapist to other therapists, Freud made clear that the particularity and limit of his method were not a result only of its scientific aspect. In seeking the origin, force, and meaning of morbid symptoms, it is a method which proceeds *per via di levare*, in the manner of sculpture; it tends to "extract something", despite the "resistance which makes the patient cling to his illness and fight against his own recovery". Quoting Hamlet, "you cannot play upon me", Freud pointed out that "it is not easy to play upon the instrument of the mind". The doctor can only avail himself of the technique after long study and practice, for discovering the unconscious is realized by entering into the heart of the psychic conflict, in spite of the continued resistance and opposition of the patient. It is because it engages with this resistance, which only the giving up of hypnotic suggestion allowed it to recognize, that the analytic method can claim to act at the deepest level and transform the patient. Freud then formulated a particularity of the method that he found himself obliged to follow for "purely subjective reasons". He stressed the subtle relation between research and therapeutics in analysis.

> Putting aside for a moment the therapeutic point of view, I may also say of it that it is the most interesting method, the only one which informs us at all about the origin and inter-relation of morbid phenomena. [*ibid.*, p. 260]

It is through abandoning the therapeutic aim in favour of a desire to know that analysis opens new perspectives on "psychical ill-being", and "it alone should be capable of leading us beyond its own limits and of pointing out the way to other forms of therapeutic influence". In this text, published in 1905 some months before the Dora case, Freud did not refer to the factor of transference that closed his account of the case because it was its defining characteristic to him, and the justification of its publication was "closely bound up with its great defect" (Freud, 1905e, p. 118). It was a question that, nevertheless, hovered over the 1904 lecture; it determined in part the subtle movement with which Freud envisaged that a new therapeutic action, yet to come, implied going beyond therapeutics.

In this respect, the very first case Lou Andreas-Salomé submitted to Freud gave rise to an interesting correspondence (Pfeiffer, 1966, pp. 68–75). Analytic knowledge led her to think that a little girl's night terrors were linked to her onanistic practices. Yet, how could she give the child access to this reason? Freud pointed out two possible ways: the shortest consisted in telling the child what was going on "with complete confidence in having guessed right"; the longer but more conclusive way being to wait until her attachment to the analyst brought her to her own confession. It was then a question of waiting and persevering, counting on the "magician Patience" to do most of the work. Lou, meanwhile took a third median route: she told the child she herself also suffered the same terrors, which had to do with the fear of being watched while asleep, the whole thing stemming from a bad habit the child had no difficulty in recognizing as her own. The symptom disappeared, the masturbation continued, and the child closed herself to any new questioning. In taking its leave, the symptom shut the door behind itself. When she told Freud, he noted that the procedure, while rendering an educative influence impossible, was "therapeutically astute". He emphasized what Andreas-Salomé had noted: "What I also found fascinating in your experience was your intuition that success spelt the end of analysis and of further development. As long as man suffers he can still accomplish something".

To penetrate into the heart of psychic conflict by means of transference has the effect that "the course of the analysis is retarded and obscured, but its existence is better guaranteed against sudden and overwhelming resistances" (Freud, 1905e, p. 119). It was Dora who taught Freud this dynamic of transference, this putting into action in which the subject can and has to replay his relations to his objects and his knowledge, and thus his relation to truth. She taught him the necessity of refining, indeed, modifying, to their mutual cost, the emergent technique of analysis. It was this case, in which dreams were central, that taught Freud that "dream-interpretation should not be pursued in analytic treatment as an art for its own sake, but that its handling should be subject to those technical rules that govern the conduct of the treatment as a whole" (Freud, 1911e, p. 94), that is, the rules concerning the handling of time and transference.

The essence of Freud's articles on technique in the years between 1910 and 1915 concerns these points, not only about what the analyst needs to know, but what his position should be in relation to knowledge and the objects of libido. In "Observations on transference love" (1915a), he formulated the fight required from the analyst to treat the transference neuroses, that "slice of real life" which is between illness and real life. It is an individual fight against the enemies of analysis, the patients, and against the forces within the analyst "which seek to drag him down from the analytic level" (*ibid.*, p. 170). This combat is paradoxical in relation to the *furor sanandi*, for it requires that the analyst lend himself to the development of a new form of neurosis, perhaps a new neurosis, the transference neurosis, and that he commit himself, like a chemist, to handling those explosive substances. An effect of the treatment, it is also the way that an analysis works. It is on the condition of maintaining this neurosis that he can operate, less like a doctor than a surgeon, less with *medicina* than with *ferrum et ignis*. Invoking the gesture of the cut in this way, Freud also invoked the not so distant past, in which the surgeon was kept socially apart from the medical profession. How and where could one learn this act? How and where did this position, which is so paradoxical in relation to the desire to heal, originate?

The didactic field

One would be forgiven for thinking that the organization of the field of training during those Berlin years was an attempt to answer those questions, but it was in fact a way of avoiding them by misrecognizing their theoretical and clinical import. Three modalities of the training were supposed to bring the analytic therapist his knowledge and know-how needed for the therapeutic act: his own analysis, the teaching of theoretical knowledge, and practice under supervision.

By comparing the training analysis, preceding the theoretical and practical *cursus*, to a novitiate, Hans Sachs, the first named training analyst, took up Freud's conception of lay analysis: he who is trained as an analyst is no longer lay, whether he is a doctor or not (Sachs, 1985). In this experience, the future analyst learns to recognize and observe what was secret and hidden "from lay eyes", that is, lay in relation to analysis: the unconscious, drives, phantasies, and the non-recognition produced by repression. It was "the only way which is somewhat sure" to prevent one turning away from the knowledge, provided by books but which we nonetheless block out: infantile sexuality, the Oedipus complex, and ambivalence in relationships. It was an operation of recognition, of familiarizing oneself with that unconscious which one would explore in others in order to evaluate its influence. These arguments in favour of training analysis were very close to the advice Freud could give in 1912. However, it is significant that the dimension of transference, specifically the transference neurosis, which is the heart of the experience, was completely misrecognized in Sach's report. For Freud, the definition of someone who was not a lay person was someone who knew the mainspring of the transference and had acquired the means to handle it.

One could impute this lacuna to the brevity of the text, but it has more to do with the very specification of an analysis as didactic. The institution of training analysis has no problem in recognizing resistance to the particular nature of analytic knowledge, but in positing itself as different, at least in principle, from a therapeutic analysis, it removes the possibility that a future analyst might experience the transference neurosis he will later have to bear from others. In so doing, one is denying the very dimension that is necessary in all analyses, and this step was not going to be without consequences for the institution.

At the end of his report, Sachs raised two questions without treating them, but which would haunt subsequent debates on training: selection of candidates and the end of the training analysis. We have seen how the choice of candidates who are not too neurotic was determined by the split between the therapeutic and the didactic. In talking about the end of the latter analyses, Sachs noted that the usual marker of an ending, the lasting disappearance of symptoms, can only be lacking or deficient in an analysis carried out as non-therapeutic. Even if he could not analyse how a training analysis deprived itself of the possibility of thinking about its end, he had touched on an impasse with his remark. Paradoxically, in all the papers on training, only that of Fenichel, on the therapeutic activity of the Polyclinic, envisaged a notion of a treatment going beyond the "success of the transference" that a reduction of symptoms constitutes. He despaired less than Horney and the authors of the "directives" of the capacity of analysis to transform what was then called "character", and which Ferenczi identified with the unconscious phantasmatic structure.

The second branch of didactics is teaching, and this was first entrusted to Abraham. It was not really a novelty, as not only did the various evening meetings of the Societies become regular lectures, but Freud had also published his war winter lectures, and Ferenczi had taught at the university. What characterized the Berlin approach was the attempt to systematize teaching, even if Franz Alexander noted that it was not without scepticism, justified by Freud's reservations on this score (Alexander, 1985, p. 142). According to him, this enterprise of systematizing was explained by rules implicit in any science. In analysis, too, the variable plasticity of concepts and their adaptation to the material was very quickly replaced by "an exact and transparent coherence" in which concepts lived "their proper lives as a Golem" and claimed "their own rights". Despite their doubts, therefore, they launched into the construction of "synthetic and coherent criteria" of this scientific psychology, criteria applicable to pathology and other domains, susceptible of preventing the violation of theory on the basis of ideological, philosophical, or moral prejudices, yet capable of leaving a place for further scientific development.

Alexander's report clearly noted that the organizational principle of the compulsory theoretical *cursus* was in conformity with medical training and aimed to teach "a kind of anatomy and physiology of the psychic apparatus". The progression was one that started from an analytic psychology of normality and dealt, after the general theory of neuroses, with particular neuroses, personality disorders, perversions, delinquency, psychoses, and the technique of the treatment. To this programme were added seminars on Freud's writings (case histories, metapsychological and technical writings), as well as courses on human sciences and the application of analysis to art and literature. The fundamental principles of this teaching, mostly addressed to candidates with a medical training, consisted in "developing their sense of psychology, which was often lacking", familiarizing them with Freud's writings, and transmitting the foundations established by experience and the "conceptual system".

After a few years of finding its way, this programme of obligatory studies was fixed between 1927 and 1929, though very soon the programme favoured by Alexander structured the lectures of Abraham and Radó, before Müller-Braunschweig introduced something called "system of psychoanalysis" for his teaching. Before 1927, the obligatory courses and the optional seminars left some space for a little bit of subjectivity of the teacher, to what is, for each, the singular point of attachment to theory. Eitingon and Simmel dealt with technique, Simmel the war neuroses, Bernfeld pedagogics, Boehm perversions; Sachs regularly dealt with the question of dreams, the human sciences, but also jokes and symbolism. Only Fenichel made a space for the second topography, and, in ten years, Sachs devoted only one seminar to transference and resistance.

If these questions were probably reserved for the "practical work" sessions or the "technical seminar", which may seem very sensible from the point of view of the divisions of the training, this division misrecognized the clinical and theoretical dimension of the transference. This lack, overlapping the founding split of the training itself, is all the more astonishing in that it coincided with a decisive theoretical advance of Freud's. It was in analysing the trait common to a traumatic neurosis (including war neuroses), a child's game, the constraints of destiny, and repetition in the transference, that he uncovered, in *Beyond the Pleasure Principle*, the repetition compulsion and the death drive. Recognizing how this theoretical invention had consequences for the treatment doubtless raised technical questions, but were they only a question of learning a technique?

The third leg of the Berlin training programme was supervised practice at the Polyclinic. There, the trainee would find a "rich source of patients" adapted to his needs by the management, in a comfortable setting protected from the isolation characteristic of private practice. According to the case, he could adapt the steps he learnt in his own training analysis using knowledge gleaned from theoretical lectures. This convergence of interests was realized in regular reports made to the director: the beginner could draw on the advice of an experienced analyst while the director could fulfil his responsibility by means of watchful supervision (Radó, 1985,

p. 147ff). In his report of 1923, Eitingon entrusted to the superviser, that is, himself, the task of detecting the "host of errors" committed by a novice. He could say, "I have supervision in hand", and maintain his right to intervene in the practice of the trainee: "we protect the patients entrusted to the trainee through the supervision we exercise over the treatment and being always ready to withdraw the case from the student and continue it ourselves". This type of intervention was not even limited to supervision, as the teaching committee also reserved the right to break off a training analysis in the case of unfavourable development.

This institution, "firmly entrenched in daily practice under the heading of 'supervision analysis'", aiming at in depth study of a case, was accompanied, after some years, by a "technical seminar", more concerned with furthering knowledge through large numbers of cases. The mutual acquaintance of each other's cases the trainees thus received completed the work of understanding in supervision with respect to diagnosis, structure of the case, and the technical process. This help and indirect supervision was a way of countering the main handicap Freud had identified in the training: that one can only know analysis "second hand", as the exchange of words that makes a treatment does not allow of either listeners or demonstration to a witness (Freud, 1915–1917, p. 15). It is only in one's own analysis that one's judgement is independent of the confidence placed in the one who informs. It is also the only access to subtleties of technique. For it is not as if the trainee analyst can get these like a trainee surgeon, by observation, gradual participation, and eventual practice under the eye of a master.

It was this particularity of analysis that led Freud to transmit the rules that he himself had learnt and modified according to his experience. In a series of articles, in his letters and meetings, he transmitted his way of doing and saying things, as well as determining the right moment for it. The technical aspects were not separable from the theoretical and clinical dimensions, and they questioned the end of analysis, as the letter to Andreas-Salomé shows, as much as the position of the analyst, specifically his position in relation to what he knows, what he has to know, and what he does not know.

One of the first exchanges with Abraham sheds light on this knotting of knowing and not-knowing. Speaking of a case of obsessional neurosis, Abraham recounted what he had been able to extract from repression, starting from a screen-memory, in only two sessions and without real resistance, but then not knowing how to advance. He asked Freud whether he could say something general about compulsions and by what means he could accede to the deeper layers. Freud answered him briefly with respect to compulsions, and then gave him two general rules.

> 1. "Take your time", in the words of the Salzburg motto. Mental changes are never quick, except in revolutions (psychoses). Dissatisfied after only two sessions. At not knowing everything! 2. A problem like: how do I go on? must not exist. The patient shows the way, in that by strictly following the basic rule (saying everything that comes into his mind) he displays his prevailing psychic surface. [Falzeder, 2002, pp. 17–21]

Abraham responded by confessing his embarrassment in having asked for help in order to obtain "a rapid analytic triumph", his hope of winning greater certainty in his practice, and his consolation in noting that things had not been much better in Freud's own work, with Dora. Did he understand how Freud's rules gave more weight to not-knowing than to the mastery of a knowledge or the certainty of a technique, to the time needed to listen to what an illness has to say than to the ritualization of certain procedures?

On completion of these three stages of the didactic *cursus*, the Teaching Commission authorized the candidate to function as practising analyst. Once he disposed of "a certain amount of personal experience", the candidate could apply to the German Psychoanalytic Society. The chronological structure of the training kept the patient, the student, and the new analyst separated. This was a break from Freud's way, of, for example, extending the rules of analysis even to work meetings, or excusing himself for treating his listeners as patients. That was due not to a confusion of place, but to a recognition of the special relation to the object that analysis involves. The inaugural split between therapeutic and training analysis, with its risk of instrumentalizing theoretical knowledge and ritualizing technique, was all the more striking for having been entrenched in a set of rules precisely during the years that Freud was struggling with the repetition compulsion, the death drive, and the negative therapeutic reaction. It is equally remarkable that the organization and rules of the training were constructed according to the logic of "an analyst is being trained", when Freud was groping for the logic of the phantasy with his article "A child is being beaten . . ." (Freud, 1919e). One could be forgiven for thinking that from that point on, analytic training and psychoanalysis followed two diverging paths and one could ask whether the very establishment of analytic training partook of the resistance of the analysts to Freud's elaborations.

BERLINER
PSYCHOANALYTISCHE POLIKLINIK

VORTRÄGE UND KURSE.

DIE BERLINER
PSYCHOANALYTISCHE VEREINIGUNG
veranstaltet in diesem Quartal folgende Vortragsreihen:

1. Dr. K. ABRAHAM:
KURS ZUR EINFÜHRUNG IN DIE PSYCHOANALYSE
(Allgemaine und spezielte Neurosenlehre, Sexualtheorie, Traumlebre usw,) mit anschließenden Besprechangen. Dienstag und Freitag 8–10 Uhr abends. Daner 6 Wochen, Beginn Freitag, 29 Oktober. Honorar für Ärzte 120 M., für Studierende der Medizin 30 M.

2. Frau Dr. K. HORNEY:
WELCHE FÄLLE AUS DER ÄRZTL. PRAXIS EIGNEN SICH ZUR PSYCHOANALYTISCHEN BEHANDLUNG?
(Kritische beiträge zur Anwendung der Psychoanalyse) 4 Vorträge, Montag, 1., 8., 15., 22. November, abends 8 Uhr. Honorar 40 M. bzw. 10 M.

3. Dr. E. SIMMEL:
ÜBER PSYCHOANALYSE DER KRIEGSNEUROSEN UND IHRER FOLGEERSCHEINUNGEN.
3 Vorträge, Sonnabend, 6., Mittwoch, 10., Sonnabend, 13. November, abends 8 Uhr. Honorar 30 M. bzw. 10 M.

4. Dr. H. LIEBERMANN:
ÜBER DEN AUFBAU DER ZWANGSNEUROSEN
(an Hand von Beispielen ans der Praxis) 4 Vorträge, Mittwoch, 17., 24. November, 1., 8. Dezember, abends 8 Uhr. Honorar 40 M. bzw. 10 M.

Außer diesen für Ärtze und Mediziner bestimmten Kursen finden noch zwei Kurse statt, welche die nichtmedizinischen Gebiete der Psychoanalyse betreffen:

5. Dr. H. SACHS (Wien):
EINFÜHRUNG IN DIE PSYCHOANALYTISCHE THEORIE,
mit besonder Berücksichtigung der Traumdeutung (12 Vorträge).

6. Dr. H. SACHS:
DIE ANWENDUNG DER PAYCHOANALYSE AUF DIE GEISTESWISSWNSCHAFTEN.

Die Vorträge finden in der Poliklinik, W., Potsdamerstraße 29/III, statt. Listen zur Einzeichnung liegen dortsebst wochentäglich vormittags aus.

Reproduced from the *Internationale Zeitschrift für Psychoanalyse*, 6, 1920.

CHAPTER THREE

The Introduction of Training: Crises and Debates

Freud's fantastical idea

"I want to feel assured that the therapy will not destroy the science". This cry of Freud's in the postscript to *The Question of Lay Analysis* (1926e) was addressed to those who misrecognize the fact that in analysis the dividing line is not between therapeutic analysis and non-therapeutic applications, but between scientific analysis and its applications, whether therapeutic or not. This shows that, having read the contributions to the debate on lay analysis, Freud's cry was addressed to most of those who intervened in the preparatory discussion to the Innsbruck conference and which "finally showed that [his] small pamphlet was not superfluous after all" (Paskaukas, 1993, p. 619).

Written "for friends" in June 1927 without intending to be published, this postscript was finally published as the closing part of the dossier (Freud, 1926e, pp. 251–258); with Jones' support, Eitingon suppressed three pages Freud had singled out, leaving it to him to decide on suppression if he judged them dangerous and apt to serve as pretext for a split of the Americans (Paskaukas, 1993, pp. 621, 623). These pages are now available thanks to the work of Grubrich-Simitis (1997, pp. 177–180).

In retrospect, this postscript sheds light on what was at stake for Freud in the text of 1926, over and above the conditions of time and place that gave rise to it. It further explains the use of the rhetorical ploy of dialogue. When Freud wrote *The Question of Lay Analysis*, he had already been in touch with the public health officials of the Vienna city council. He had met with Arnold During, and written for him an evaluation of the practice of analysis by non-physicians; he had asked Julius Tandler to review the decision to forbid Theodor Reik from practising analysis. Soon after, he had addressed a notice to the *Neue Freie Presse*. The scope and ambition of the text in "showing what analysis is and what demands it makes on the analyst . . . the relations, far from simple, between analysis and medicine", go beyond the steps taken to support "an analyst trained in [his] school" in the legal proceedings started against him (Freud, 1926i, p. 248). If he could say in 1927 that "his text served no purpose", that he did not succeed in unifying the position of analysts, only demonstrates that the text of 1926 was addressed to analysts as much as to the powers of the day. In 1926, Freud was aware of the tensions concerning admission of lay candidates and the selection of candidates for training (Schröter, 1996); he could not have forgotten that Reik's analyst, Abraham, was opposed to his admission and that he, Freud, had supported him (Reik, 1953). The impersonal interlocutor with whom he engages in dialogue could thenceforth be seen as a condensation of two people: one, a scientist responsible for public health, and the other a medical analyst in favour of keeping analysis contained within the medical profession. Freud opposes him with the good faith, honesty, and culture necessary to listen to what is novel about analysis and to admit the conclusions one has to draw from it concerning the training and qualification of the analyst.

One could also see the interlocutor as a means of self-critique, or even a hesitation of Freud's on this issue; but the postscript and the letters show he was not really divided about it. The choice of dialogue shows his prudence and skill in taking the more radical position of favouring the practice of analysis by non-physicians, without complementary medical training. Yet, the theatricality of the staging (facial expressions, asides) goes beyond the tradition of dialogue, which itself runs from Plato through Rousseau via Fénelon, certain forms of transmission in Jewish tradition, or the protocols of the pastoral visits of certain churches. One could therefore argue that at the moment Freud was faced with a crisis which threatened to lead to a new split, his rhetorical choice bore witness to a fantasy of unification of the movement based on the recognition of the specificity of a new profession, able to develop "the most suitable training" for its practice. But the forces of division were stronger than this fantasy, and Freud did not let the dialogue end with an agreement between him and the interlocutor. In reality, the civil authorities were less deaf to his arguments than the analysts. Reik was not convicted, but Freud's position was not taken up by the other analysts.

Jones had been right about Freud's intentions (Paskaukas, 1993, p. 605). His first criticism of *The Question of Lay Analysis* was that the text went beyond the concise argumentation needed by the Viennese authorities, and that it avoided the technical discussion necessary with the real interlocutors, that is, the practising analysts. With some skill, he separated out in the text the "ingenious" exposition of what analysis is, the "rather weak" argument on lay analysis, and the remarkable vision of the future. In his critical review, as well as in his contributions to the discussions, Jones was concerned to counter Freud's arguments, which he found partial and hasty. The final vision of an independent discipline and profession founded on a suitable training derive, for him, from a "music of the future" (*Zukunftsmusik*); he praised this wager and this idea "the imagination can seize upon", but did not let himself be seduced, for his own task lay in reconciling loyalty to analysis with his loyalty to medicine. But can one really separate the three strands of Freud's text without misrecognizing its movement of demonstration, without flattening the doctrinal dimension on what analysis is, and what it is that qualifies one to apply it to technical or political questions? Freud thought that it was indeed from theory that one could deduce what one wanted from the patient, how one attained this goal, and the specific modalities of training required by both theory and practice. But analytic doctrine cannot be transmitted only by theoretical teaching; the conviction of the rightness of the theory is only acquired in the crucible of one's own analysis, in one's own body and soul. However dogmatic it tries to be, the exposition of doctrine has to take that particularity into account; and this is what Freud did with his dialogue.

Ferenczi thought this text was essential reading for anyone wishing to learn the essentials of analysis; Anna Freud thought it was even more useful than the *Introductory Lectures*, and proposed to place it as an introduction and to use the sequence of its themes for a new edition of selected works; Jones recognized that there Freud gave "the best description of what analysis is, its theory and practice" (Grubrich-Simitis, 1997, p. 233; Paskaukas, 1993, op. cit.). He marvelled at its ingeniousness. More than ingeniousness, however, what is at work in this text is a way of going forward with, rather than against, the resistance to analysis, using it to overcome it, in a way that is homologous to the way the treatment works, particularly with the resistance that determines transference. That was the path chosen by Freud to teach his interlocutor what analysis teaches, what an analyst must know in order to treat these patients who are so unlike any others, and how he could learn to do this. In this way, the dimension of sexuality, of Oedipus, and the primacy of the phallus, only make an appearance in the fourth chapter, when the interlocutor asks about the rumour that analysis is concerned with "the most intimate and the most disgusting matters", arguing that these must surely be matters for physicians only. As in the treatment, Freud simply waited patiently for the interlocutor to broach the question.

This same expository concern, conforming to the history of the development of the concepts rather than a system, yet aiming also to dramatize the material, led Freud to hold back an important part of the psychical apparatus right until the fifth chapter. When the interlocutor has admitted that the knowledge necessary to practise analysis entailed very little medical knowledge, lots of psychology, and again a little bit of biology and sexual science, when he has acknowledged that the attuned ear and tact necessary for timely interpretations require that the analyst be analysed "to the end", Freud imparts to him "the strangest thing": due to a tenacious and unconscious feeling of guilt, the neurotic does not want to be cured. That is when he formulated the hardest task of all, before which "the tasks of interpretation melt away", the task requiring the greatest level of technique and "which differentiates the analytic method from all other psychotherapeutic procedures": handling the transference. Only then did Freud explain the theory of the superego, of the plurality of resistances, and of the repetition compulsion, in order to explain this paradoxical therapy in which, to get the better of negative therapeutic reaction, one has to "drive out one form of illness with another", "transform every neurosis, whatever its content into a condition of pathological love". There is no other way than through this transference neurosis to "correct" the first repressions and repetition (Freud, 1926e, pp. 218–228). Only this deserves to be called analysis.

This paradox, the skill, the patience, calm, and forbearance required from the analyst seem to win over the interlocutor: "Tell me only how and where I can learn what is necessary to practise analysis." Freud first answered factually that two, and soon three, institutes would dispense a theoretical teaching, ensure the analysis of future analysts as well as the supervision of their first practical steps, while practical experience and exchange of ideas within the analytic societies would complete what was lacking in this first training. Freud could then introduce a subtle twist: he who has grasped what can be taught of the theory of the unconscious, who has acquired the delicate technique of interpretation, the fight against resistance, and the handling of the transference, "someone like that is no longer lay in the field of analysis". He is qualified to undertake a treatment, whereas an untrained doctor is still lay with respect to analysis.

The interlocutor, impartial but still in favour of a medical monopoly of analytic practice, agreed without, however, giving up: what Freud had presented was just a new medical speciality, requiring, in fact, a specific training found only in those institutes. The new line of argument begun here was criticized by Jones, not without reason, for its weakness. Freud was suggesting that prior medical training, with its emphasis on physical factors, went against what the future analyst needed, and that medicine did not recognize the unilaterality of the science of the unconscious or the authority of the institutes. He also argued that the embarrassment a neurotic constituted for the art of medical healing and the low expectation of success in therapy ("the real remedy is death") encouraged medical charlatanism in analytic matters. At the same time, he could not yet define what sort of "definitive training" could give the right to practise: "I have not resolved this and am not sure I ever will". Reading between the lines, there is an acknowledgement here that analytic institutes do not contradict the idea of a medical speciality and could even be dedicated to it. One could speculate that Freud's fervent denunciation of the *furor prohibendi* and the bureaucratic leanings which followed in the text was addressed, unwittingly or not, as much to the institutes' obsession with rules as to the administrative authorities in Vienna, always ready to block the way to intellectual freedom and to "the impartial desire to know" (*unparteiische Wissbegierde*).

Yet, the very weakest link in Freud's argument is revealed only in the last chapter, after the interlocutor has brought up the diversity of opinion among Freud's followers. Freud first linked this to "the grip of esprit de corps", but had to recognize that analytical theory cannot answer the medical argument concerning the suitability for analysis, that is, the differential diagnosis between neurosis and mental illness. At a time when the causes of an "inhibition of the ego" were as yet unknown to analytic theory, and given the hypothesis of a non-psychogenic aetiology for certain neuroses, Freud held back from entrusting the differential diagnosis and those treatments to non-physicians, reserving the prerogative for doctors. He denied, however, that one had to be a doctor to deal with physical symptoms that might appear during an analysis, because even a physician analyst would have had to have them referred to another doctor. He continued by making discreet but firm corrections to the practices being institutionalized in the institutes. On the one hand, he indicated that it was only analysis which allowed one to assess personal aptitude for practising such a demanding activity; on the other, he asserted that training analysts, who could be lay analysts, should also conduct therapeutic analyses to complete their own training. Once again, he was in favour of freedom of movement and the absence of unnecessary restrictions.

Having arrived at that point, Freud gave free rein to a "fantastical" idea: if one were to found a college (*Hochschule*) of analysis, one would teach not only depth psychology, an introduction to biology, to the clinical aspects of psychiatry, and a large part of the science of sexuality, but also the history of civilization, mythology, the psychology of religious sciences, and literature. For the experience of the analyst leads him into another world, with different phenomena and different laws than those taught by the medical faculty. This experience, which renders these two orders of knowledge necessary, is the experience of the "chasm separating the physical from the psychical". It is doubtless this chasm which makes analysis, like the neurotic, an embarrassment, and risks making "its last resting-place in a text-book of psychiatry under the heading 'Methods of Treatment'" (Freud, 1926e, p. 248). Far from such a resting-place, the future will perhaps show that the application of analysis to the therapy of neuroses is not its most important application, that it will be less important than its use in "all the sciences which are concerned with the evolution of human civilization and its major institutions such as art, religion and the social order" (*ibid.*). These were the very applications of analysis pursued by Freud in his Wednesday evening meetings, in *Imago*, and in a number of his works.

The 1927 debate on lay analysis

The contributions to the debate of 1927 on lay analysis show the extent of the misunderstanding between Freud and most analysts, as well as the extent to which his "fantastical" idea for training fell on deaf ears. (*The International Journal* [Parts 2 and 3 of volume VIII] and the *Internationale Zeitschrift* [Parts 1, 2, and 3 of volume XIII], see Schneider.) Only the Hungarian Psychoanalytical Association collectively adopted this position, considered the issue resolved, and denounced the hidden motives and resistance at work in the offensive against lay analysts; for them, the essential problem was the training, the core of which was one's own analysis. Those in support of medical training, when not relying on a corporate logic that misrecognized the specificity of these patients so unlike others and of this treatment not like any other, based their positions on the argument of diagnostics and recurrent symptoms. Only Simmel tried to tackle this second point from the perspective of repetition and the handling of the transference. Several analysts argued for the clinical wisdom of doctors, their familiarity with the experience of life and death. Some interventions evinced the hope that analysis would allow medicine to continue to fulfil its therapeutic task.[1] Ignoring the chasm between corporeal and psychical that Freud had emphasized, Alexander dreamt of a "unified science capable of understanding and healing humanity in the unity of body and mind"; he hoped a time would come in which a lay analyst and a doctor untrained in analysis would be transitory phenomena of the past. Several analysts recognized the contribution of lay analysts to applied analysis and to the scientific dimension of analysis. But it was the lay analysts who contested the dividing line between applied analysis and therapeutic analysis. Roheim made clear that a therapeutic practice is necessary for the training of an ethnologist who aims to apply analysis to his science; Sachs spoke of the unfounded nature of the division itself: as a training analysis progresses, the character anomalies, the inhibitions, and emotional troubles reveal themselves with a seriousness equal to that of a therapeutic analysis.

Jones' lengthy contribution was intended to situate itself above emotion and passion, due, according to him, to the transitional period in which analysis found itself, and adopted the same vantage point as Freud's text with respect to the future. To this end, he defined the new and immense task of the movement: to organize analytic knowledge. Apparently ignoring Freud's incessant theoretical advances, or judging them unsuitable for "an organised and verifiable body of knowledge", he considered that this task had been neglected until now and that neurotic interest in analysis was no longer enough to accomplish the task. It had to be carried out as much in the training as in its relation to other sciences. A discussion on the "appropriate training" was not on the cards, however: the *cursus* and selection were, for Jones, technical problems reserved for the International Training Committee. Nor was the relation to other sciences really elaborated. The work of presentation and systematic classification of concepts needed to avoid the charge of being esoteric, so analysis would need a body of researchers trained scientifically. This would allow one to escape the "hothouse atmosphere" conducive to sectarian jealousies. To this end, it seemed evident to Jones that the closest and most promising point of contact with science was medicine, that "neighbouring science" which had the additional advantage of protecting against intellectualization. He did not really engage in the methodological reflection of a Müller-Braunschweig, which led the latter to consider that not only do natural sciences not have a monopoly on empirical observation, but that the science of language, for example, is more suited for grasping the causal relation or the relation of meaning between a symptom, or any other substitute formation, and what is really in question.

What mattered to Jones was to justify the position that analysis could not be an independent profession. He understood that

Freud's position, which he thought extreme, implied this independence, and wrote to him that he had a lot to say on the subject (Paskaukas, 1993, p. 605). He understood the novelty of the social bond Freud invented with analysis. But he thought of this novelty in terms of a profession. Rejecting both the prohibition of lay analysis as " an act of pure tyranny" and the Freudian thesis that medicine is indifferent, even unnecessary, to the practice of analysis, he took up an intermediate position, the only one, according to him, which respected the interests of analysis, of analysts, and of patients. Only a medical training, prior or complementary, would guarantee recognition of analysis by science and the greater public; by avoiding diagnostic errors and the risks of inhibition in the course of the treatment, it gave greater authority to the analyst; last, it would also prevent taking mental illness out of the medical sphere.

By undoing the logical unity between the physical and the psychical, a unity necessary to tackle human suffering, independent lay practice would produce a divorce between analysis and clinical medicine that would be as harmful to the one as to the other. If medicine were not to retain the prerogative of diagnosis and prescription, even if delegating care to assistants, mental illness would cease to be the object of medicine. If the development of an independent profession would seem to benefit patients by leading to lower fees, it would be at the risk of no longer being able to distinguish it from wild analysis. Therefore, it mattered to Jones that the International Training Committee, founded two years previously on his initiative, create and organize a medical discipline, encouraging lay people into medical training and rigorously selecting those who would judge this complementary *cursus* inopportune.

It is difficult to know with Jones what had the upper hand, his social and professional view of analysis or his view of analytic knowledge and its organization. This conception of knowledge, shared by most of those who undertook to institutionalize training along the lines of a division between training and therapeutic analysis, shows a misunderstanding of Freud and a misrecognition of the path he set out in his text. All of the contributions ignored the long path Freud had to walk to uncover the finality of analysis and the training required for it. Far from instrumentalizing analytic knowledge for the use of a therapeutic end external to it, Freud based his idea of the end of analysis and of the training of the analyst from the perspective of open-ended unfinished knowledge. It is from the theory developed to account for the formation of symptoms and the negative therapeutic reaction, that is, the theory of repression, the drives, and repetition, that he derived the aim of correcting repression and repetition. It was a procedure he would not budge from. When confronted with the demands of a practice restricted to training analyses and serious illnesses, it was starting from "the Witch Metapsychology" that he would rewrite, in 1937, "the proper action of analytic therapy": the retroactive correction of the primary processes of repression. That is where the theory led and one could not renounce this aim, even if experience did not allow one to decide if it could be realized. "Without metapsychological speculation and theorising—I had almost said 'phantasying'—we shall not get another step forward" (Freud, 1937c, p. 225).

In the postscript he wrote for his colleagues after having read the contributions, Freud asked himself how one could persist in denying that analysis was a non-medical practice and questioned the "project of seduction" operated by medicine: was it an attempt at appropriation that conserved or destroyed its object? He noted that, in his own case, the weakness of his sadistic disposition had instead meant that the derivative of this disposition, which consists in helping others, did not have to develop. The triumph of his life was, therefore, to have corrected the deviation from the original aims which the long detour through medicine had been, and that his need to understand the enigmas of the world had in the end been successful. He criticized the contributions for needlessly overestimating the difficulties of diagnosis and occasional physical symptoms and for misrecognizing that the analyst's authority derives from the transference rather than from medical knowledge. It seems a shame that Lou Andreas-Salomé was not present at this debate in 1927. She might have been able to communicate what she had already formulated in her journal of 1912: it had to be a physician, the person who knew how to balance life, like another egg of Columbus, on the broken fulcrum of psychical suffering. By catching that life, ready to escape into the organic "by the coat-tails", Freud had managed to "put it to the question", he had known how to "squeeze" the psychical between the ungraspable of being-alive and its dismembered elements, until then seen merely as a degradation of the physical (Andreas-Salomé, 1965, p. 40). Freud tried to make it clear that it had to be a doctor separated from medical tradition.

Freud had heard Jones' threat that medicine might lose the monopoly on dealing with mental illness after having spent so long securing this privilege. Borrowing an argument from Reik, he responded by saying that medicine does not have the monopoly on psychotherapy, as is shown by the Protestant tradition of soul healing or Adlerian therapies. But, in opposition to these psychotherapeutic practices, which relieve by restoring religiosity or an interest in the community, psychoanalysis deprives itself of these methods, as it deprived itself of hypnosis, and chooses the difficult path of confronting, by means of the transference neurosis, repression and repetition. In 1928, he asked Oskar Pfister whether he grasped the secret link existing between *The Question of Lay Analysis* and *The Future of an Illusion*; he was reaffirming his wish to protect analysis not only against doctors, but also against priests (Freud & Pfister, 1963). The exchanges in 1927 allow us to see that it was not only the social respectability of analysis which was at stake in the question of lay analysis, but that the novelty of analysis shook up the relatively recent appropriation of mental illness by medicine. The works of Michel Foucault and Jan Goldstein on the genealogy and history of this appropriation throw light on those particular aspects of the debate (Foucault, 1961; Goldstein, 1997).

Freud did not ignore these social and professional considerations; he just did not give in to them. In the postscript, not published by Jones and Eitingon but now accessible, he clearly showed his desire to explain what social, economic, and ideological logic governs the American position. The uncovering of their motivations did not make him more understanding, and he explained their position as an attempt at repression (Freud, 1926e, pp. 251–258). According to him, no practical consideration whatever should prevail over the "scientific gain" which is the most "joyful" aspect of analytic work. Nothing should endanger what made his procedure unique: "the close union between treatment and research". Freud had, indeed, a very early awareness of the conflict between therapeutics and research in analysis. Lou Andreas-Salomé related that his last conversation with her at the end of her stay in Vienna referred to this; she described how Freud insisted on the necessity that a researcher always stay in close contact with the material from patients. Only such contact allowed analytic research to work while staying in the domain of the unconscious, giving truly new results and opening unnoticed doors. Without it, analytic research would, like the dream, disappear without hope of return (Andreas-Salomé, 1965, pp. 139–131). In the postscript, Freud even went as far as to say that, since a neurotic offered more instructive material than a normal person, he represented a good half of the training possibilities to whoever wanted to learn and apply analysis to therapeutics or to other research. Once more considering "the most appropriate training" (1926e, p. 252), Freud reckoned that "a scheme of training for analysts has still to be created" (ibid.). He gave guidelines as to what might contribute to it: the sciences of the mind, psychology, the history of civilization, sociology, anatomy, biology, the history of evolution. It was an ideal to be sure, but one that "can and must be realised"; the training institutes are a beginning for such a project "in spite of all their youthful insufficiencies" (ibid.).

Freud did not greatly appreciate the fact that Jones put the issue of lay analysis on the agenda of a debate in the different societies prior to the Congress; he would have preferred that the whole association adopt his viewpoint and its requirements. He would have preferred unanimity on an issue which concerned analysis as such. He also wished to protect the analyst's freedom to emigrate at will. Instead, he had to recognize that the authority needed for general agreement was lacking and that separation from the Americans was on the cards (Freud, letter to Eitingon dated 22 March 1927, quoted in Jones, 1957, p. 316). The New York Society's unilateral decision to condemn lay analysis affected Freud to the point where he could not face reading Eitingon's resolution for the Congress and, having written his postscript, he turned away from the issue: "I have exerted myself to the utmost but have obtained little and can do no more" (Falzeder & Brabant, 1996, 1099F). In 1927, a split thus emerged between Freud and the movement he had wanted to organize to give a home to analytic research. This split is also the one between the isolation of "a commander-in-chief without an army" supported only by Ferenczi, and the political realism of Jones, who, more pragmatic and understanding of local situations, had taken over as political head.

The crisis Freud precipitated around the issue of lay analysis gave Jones the chance to use his talent and taste for organizing the movement. The organization of training was to be a masterpiece of compromise between centralism and local prerogatives. After the Congress, he explained to Freud his strategy for pacifying the Americans: to fight against "wild training" (*wilde Ausbildung*) by being draconian in the selection of candidates and in respecting the norms of training committees. Freud responded laconically that "the whole organisation was after all still quite young and untested" (Paskaukas, 1993, pp. 625, 633). He considered this evolution "fateful" for the future of analysis (Freud's letters to Ferenczi dated 22 April and 13 May 1928, quoted in Jones, 1957, pp. 319–320). He could not have imagined that part of the "gloomy future" that awaited analysis "if it did not succeed in creating an abode for itself outside of medicine" was going to be the serious and sometimes fatal difficulty of integration in certain host countries for analysts obliged to leave their country because of the Nazis.

Questioning the standard

The Wiesbaden Congress of 1932 marked the failure of Freud to unify the movement around his position, but it also marked Eitingon's failure to unify it around the median position of Jones, which would have meant a non-independent lay practice and therefore also allowing a lay training under strict conditions. In 1929, Eitingon had tried to convince his colleagues that the cohesion of the community, necessary to preserve the integrity of analysis, demanded the sacrifice of individual positions; he had pleaded for the enlargement of the circle of those admitted into therapeutic work and stressed that the positions taken on this would affect the destiny of psychoanalysis (Eitingon, 1929, p. 511). In 1932, Jones' politics of compromise saved the integrity of the Association, but at the price of a general rule for the selection of candidates and therefore leaving each society free to make its own decision regarding lay analysis.

It is tempting to say that "of course" Freud failed completely, and it is important to grasp the consequences of this failure.[2] What Freud attempted with *The Question of Lay Analysis* was to show that the most appropriate training for an analyst is determined by the aims and specific practice of the treatment, which are themselves determined by analytic theory, by those constructions that, based on experience, circumscribe what can be called analysis and what should be called by another name. It made training a doctrinal question, on which technical steps and procedures depended. As in 1914, when Adler and Jung split, Freud, in 1926, put forward his authority at the risk of disagreeing with those he had secretly installed as guardians of doctrine, risking, in fact, a split with a part of the Association. It is probably not insignificant that, in a letter of 23 September 1927, he called Jones to account for his behaviour (was he a double agent for the Americans?), concerning a campaign he accused him of waging against Anna Freud's child analysis, and on his tolerance with respect to the erroneous views of Joan Riviere. In the same letter, Freud brought up the letter in which he had written to Brill "we should lose nothing as colleagues, or on a scientific or material level, if they wanted to recede", leaving to later historical development the question of judging between the divergent opinions on technique of the two child analysts, and, finally, finding heretical the way Joan Riviere "derealised" analysis, although without seeking to discourage her. It meant that he could differentiate in the various possible disagreements between what was an unbiased theoretical discussion, one justifying special caution, and, one meriting separation (Paskaukas, 1993, pp. 623–625). The letter demonstrates the kind of authority Freud had first tried to transfer to Jung and the International Association, "an authority capable of giving instructions and warnings", capable of safeguarding the future of analysis (Freud, 1914d, p. 43). Jones' answer, and the ensuing correspondence about Riviere, show how difficult it was to register these distinctions, as well as what a dead-end it was to try to institute this authority in a place of power.

The fact that the Wiesbaden report on admission and training was carried unanimously shows that Freud's authority was not recognized on an issue affecting psychoanalysis and its future. The political and technical answer Jones gave left it to the local training committees to define their orientation concerning the selection of non-medics. It defined the prerogative of the International Committee: standardizing the training. Training analyses could only be conducted by authorized trainers, selection had to take the candidate's personality into account, candidates promised not to declare themselves analysts without authorization from the training committee, lay candidates promised not to set up an independent practice, a proper training entailed a training analysis, then two years of theory, then two supervisions for at least a year.

During the Oxford Congress in 1929, Eitingon had argued that those charged with training were the guardians of the integrity of analysis, since scientific research risked being received in piecemeal fashion by the public and distorted to the point of misrecognition. He rejoiced in the fact that, through mutual influence rather than discussion, all the centres followed the same path in "a logical and beautiful systematicness". Soon after the crisis around Rank's heterodoxy, which shook the Secret Committee, the International Training Committee thus took on the task of guardian of doctrine. This attribution was all the more surprising because, as Jones would reproach them in 1936, Eitington and the Committee did not really bother basing the procedures they organized and instituted on sound theory. Thus, what began to emerge was an orthopraxis, coexisting with a doctrinal pluralism not yet recognized as such, something confirmed at Wiesbaden as the consequence of the rejection of Freud's position. The American offensive of 1938 against the International Training Committee was its logical consequence: after the Oxford clause, by means of which American societies could refuse affiliation to analysts trained in Europe, after the Wiesbaden compromise, the very existence of the Committee began to be contested. From 1932 on, a period of local control and doctrinal pluralism, training became a power issue in the transmission of analysis and an occasion for splits. It was in 1936 that the IPV became the International Psychoanalytic Association.

The question of lay analysis became a cause for a split in the Netherlands, Switzerland, and California; the other splits were played out around other theoretical and technical questions. Each training committee inherited the double task of guaranteeing the orthodoxy of what was being taught and presenting students with the new developments in theory and technique. The five splits affecting the American Societies between 1941 and 1947 shed light on how the tension between these two objectives was dealt with by means of disciplinary proceedings and violent splits, all the more difficult to treat in that transference relations were at play

(Thompson, 1995). The British case established the reputation of their Society to contain, if not the individual dissidents, at least the collective movements that were in conflict. What made it a "case" was the way in which an agreement was reached in 1946 after the Anna Freud–Melanie Klein controversies—the *gentleman's agreement*, or *Ladies' agreement*—to organize the lectures and the supervisions in the training according to a doctrinal pluralism. A distribution of the lectures and supervision sessions between the three currents in the society governed the delicate interlinking of three problems: the compatibility of Kleinian theories with Freudian ones, the opportunity to transmit them to students and, therefore, the selection of training analysts, and the positions of power and influence in the Society. The agreement was reached at the risk of rendering the Society sclerotic by closing it to further debate. The menacing context of the war, the exile of Freud's family, and the proximity of his death were major factors in this singular result, which Jones' pragmatism, the English political tradition, and the group of Independents might not have solved by themselves. Anna Freud explained her refusal to split in terms of her gratitude for the welcome the British Psychoanalytical Society had given to her, to Freud, and to the analysts fleeing the Nazis (Hinshelwood, 1995; King, 1981).

It was no doubt logical that the first voice raised in opposition to this system of training was that of Balint. Trained in Berlin, he was an analyst in Budapest during the time that the analytic society there opposed the temporality of the *cursus* of training and the conception of supervision that followed from it; exiled in London, he participated as an Independent in the *Controversial Discussions*. It was not without disquiet that, as a trainer himself, he communicated to his colleagues, as well as the students present at his lecture (which was an innovation), his criticisms of the terrible state of affairs regarding training (Balint, 1948). The absence of any publications for more than twenty years was testimony to the inhibition of thought of the trainers as well as the lack of any scientific discussion of the aims and methods of the training; the control of training analyses and supervisions was the effect of a dogmatism which did not take analytic experience into account. The submission of the students to this system could be seen in the way they were herded into "genetic groups" around a master. Balint proposed a diagnosis for these symptoms: analytic training had taken the form of primitive initiation ceremonies: esoteric knowledge, dogmatic exposés, authoritarian techniques, submission to, and identification with, the initiator on the part of candidates. Contrary to the official aim of analysis to produce a strong and critical ego, training had become the "formation of a superego". The work under supervision and the *ex cathedra* teaching seemed to him particularly propitious to this formation of a superego, all the more so in so far as the competition between the schools of thought encouraged each to train as many candidates as possible and to turn them into loyal pupils.

This crucial aspect of training—its initiatory character—which is clearly visible in the history of training, which he proposed to divide into periods, was, for Balint, an effect of the esoteric dimension of this history. To make an identification with the trainer the principle of the system of training was derived from the esoteric goal of the training, which itself aimed to realize Freud's concern to institute an authority "capable of giving instructions and warnings". Balint linked this process with both the initiatory model and with the ecclesiastical model, in which infallibility, even though denied by Freud, was delegated to the disciples close to the Secret Committee, thus establishing an "apostolic succession" from one generation to another. But he did not question the links he made between the three models of initiation, apostolic succession, and filiation, or the ones he described between analytic authority, paternal authority, doctrinal authority, and institutional power. By questioning the standardized length of the training analysis, he came close to Ferenczi's position, to whom a training analysis was just an analysis. By contesting the principle of a chronology in training and its separation of training analysis from supervision, he went back to the Hungarian position, which gave analysis itself responsibility for analysing the countertransference and, thus, gave the concomitant task of supervision to the analyst. What he did not question was the Berlin separation between training and therapeutic analyses, nor did he reopen the doctrinal issue of lay analysis.

A few months prior to his death in 1952, Bernfeld resigned from the Teaching Commission of the San Francisco Society, speaking of his scepticism and asking whether one was really obliged to invent the least favourable situation for the teaching of psychoanalysis (Bernfeld, 1962). His lecture created a scandal, and was only published ten years later. Emphasizing, as Balint had done, that Freud, to the consternation of the "authorities", never submitted to the teaching rationalization of the professional schools that the Institutes had become, he denounced the conformism and infantilism that resulted from them. The kind of "contract" that ruled them, to wit, the promise of prestige and money represented by the diploma, produced jealousy and competition. In conformity with his lifelong interest in the impact of analysis on education and pedagogics, he proposed to centre the teaching relation on the student and not the teacher.

Although Bernfeld's proposition of a simple change in method misunderstood the difficulties relating to the nature of the object at play in the training, he raised decisive questions. Can a training analysis be institutionalized? He recognized the necessity of such an analysis, even if Freud encouraged him to practise before having done an analysis himself. But to institutionalize it and subject it to rules imposed the demands of the institution and misrecognized the fact that the need for a long and profound analysis was only an issue when the question of possible "vocation" really came up. Can one be an analyst and decide on the moment when one's analysand is ready to follow seminars, have supervision, and become an analyst, without practising a non-Freudian, even deviationist, technique? Yet, that is the institutional duty of the didactician, which, therefore, ceases to be a simple "element of the transference" and becomes an element of the patient's reality.

Can this "twisted transference situation" allow a convincing analysis of the transference, which is the only reason to justify the importance given to a personal analysis? The worst feature of this aberration is the fact that training analysts have a position of power in the Society, and can therefore designate both teachers and supervisors. Bernfeld noted that Sachs renounced any position in the Society very quickly, refusing to associate his transference authority to power and to the authority of a political position.

In 1939, Sachs had invited analysts to ponder the possible destiny of Freud's discovery of the unconscious and the Oedipus complex from the perspective of Freud's last book, *Moses and Monotheism* (Sachs, 1939). If one is forced to consider the sequence of a disappearance, an inversion, and a return of Freud's discovery, it was because of the separation that had taken place between the scientific aims of analysis and the organization of the movement. Set up at first to shelter a research menaced by the intense resistance it provoked, once it had to regulate the training and the setting up of analysts in practice, the Association became conservative, concerned with its own survival, and directed to practical ends which distanced it from its initial research aims. In a posthumously published article of 1947, Sachs took up the two problems he had raised in 1930: selection of candidates and the end of the training analysis (Sachs, 1947). He contested the separation between therapeutic and training analyses by noting that, at the current stage of civilization, psychoneurotic tendencies were universal and that the interest shown in them was usually motivated by personal problems. Furthermore, the analyst should not conduct an analysis by fixing a therapeutic or didactic aim, but solely work towards uncovering the unconscious. Though he did not ignore the contraindications of serious cases (severe obsessional neurosis, psychotic tendencies, psychopathology, perversions), he contested the postulate of normality and held that, paradoxically, certain well-adapted people without symptoms were unsuited to becoming analysts, their narcissistic rigidity keeping them removed from their own and other people's unconscious (this comment is fleshed out in Gitelson, 1954). The only specific qualification other than seriousness, honesty, and culture, relevant for any psychotherapist, paediatrician, or cleric, was that a person could face their own unconscious. The delicate problem at that point would be how to assess the "blind spots", the resistance points powerful enough to inhibit intimate knowledge of the unconscious or compromise scientific objectivity. Only analysis was able to judge of this. One could, on the other hand, refuse admission to those motivated only by financial gain or those who, moved by *furor sanandi*, wanted quick-fix psychotherapies.

Sachs thought that if an analyst definitely needed to have gained an intimate and intense understanding of the nature, language, and mechanisms of the unconscious, he certainly did not need to claim to have explored all the material, resolved all conflicts, and removed all resistance. He was on the side of Freud rather than Ferenczi, emphasizing that the end of analysis was a beginning and insisting on the need for the analyst to recognize his limits and lacks. Yet, in keeping with his reputation for telling Jewish jokes, he ended his article with a parable that Freud had used for similar questions: as Australian grouse could not be eaten freshly killed, it was first buried in a hole covered with twigs; on being taken out after six weeks it was no longer edible and fit only for the rubbish heap. This tale, which does not fail to evoke the *sicut palea* of St Thomas taken up by Lacan *à propos* of the same question, becomes even more significant when linked to another Jewish story, with which Sachs illustrated Freud's position and the inscription of his discovery in the tradition of Torah. A driver whipping his horse mercilessly answered his friends begging him to spare the animal: "As he has decided to be a horse he has to run" (*As es sich hat unternummen ze syn a Ferd, muss es leifen*). "Since we have decided to be men . . .", Sachs added (1945, p. 150). These two fables are a good introduction to the dimension of the signifier and its object, which would allow Lacan to develop, in a different setting, the questions transmitted by analysts for whom experience spoke louder than any standard.

The French Crisis of 1953

Did the regulations of a training committee ever find a more eloquent pen to prove their doctrinal foundation than that of Lacan in 1949 (Miller, 1976)? With the suspension of the *Revue française de psychanalyse* and the closing of the Institute, the Société Psychanalytique de Paris (SPP) had stopped its public activities during the war, refusing the dreadful "salvage" operation into which the Deutsche Psychoanalytische Gesellschaft had ventured with Jones' support. Soon after it had restarted its activities, the SPP delegated its training function to a Teaching Commission. Lacan's text, establishing its "regulations and doctrine", subordinated the dimension of rules to the "Freudian orthodoxy" in its relation to a "pure technique". The bureaucratic standard gained the dignity of a "regular transmission" in which "didactic experience", that is, the experience of resistance and transference in the analysis "called training", took on the status of the "fundamental rule" that Ferenczi had given it in the training of the analyst.

In one sense, the text was in conformity with the "continuous tradition" of training set up following the Berlin model; adopted by the SPP, it was published, unsigned, in September 1949 in the *Revue française de psychanalyse*. In his presentation of the themes of the statutes, which he proposed to the new Institute in November 1952, Sacha Nacht borrowed certain phrases from it. Yet, this text contained the seeds of a subversion which was its true signature and which would find its effective culmination in Lacan's "excommunication" in 1964. It was a subversion which dragged him into a split he never wanted. Far from being reducible to an orthopraxis, "pure technique" is, according to the text, the one that respects "all registers of the personality, barring none of its antinomies", remaining true to the "vicissitudes of the case"; it is in relation to this pure technique that "Freudian orthodoxy" has a meaning and is radically different from a "theory fixed into dogmas". The study of the qualifications to be looked for in candidates, while spelling out the disqualifying deficiencies and recognizing "limits inherent in any action on one's counterparts", recommended looking beyond "the sometimes precarious conditions determining the equilibrium of the biographical moment in which the candidate presents himself". Lacan insisted on "cultural training" (as much in the candidate's way of speaking as in their "fruitful kernel of knowledge") and reduced their prior professional qualifications to the status of the testimony they could give of "the subject's assimilation to human reality". If medical, and specifically psychiatric, qualifications were most desirable, the text recognized the value of other work experience and specified that "no degree of technical formation will be denied to non-medical analysts, or as one says abroad, lay analysts". In this rather subtle way, by making of training the privileged field for pure technique, the text aimed to reduce the gap between therapeutic and training analyses. The responsibility of the analyst was accentuated: the student "was put entirely under his tutelage".

With the publication of the essential documents of the split of 1953, as well as the historical work of Elisabeth Roudinesco, we are in a better position to identify how certain impasses in the training model adopted by the IPA precipitated the French institutional crisis (Miller, 1976; *Analytica*, 1978; Roudinesco, 1990). We refer the reader to those documents and that historical work and will only emphasize a few aspects of a split which, while inscribed in the logic of the IPA training, was the moment of birth of another logic of training. The doctrinal issues were not explicit factors in it, even though the group was characterized by "an absolute lack of doctrinal coherence and technique" (Miller, 1976, p. 133). The World Congress of Psychiatry of 1950 already showed an opposition between French analysts and American trends; during the trial begun in 1951 against a female lay analyst, a member of the SPP, for the illegal practice of medicine, one could have thought a coexistence was possible between adherents of medical analysis independent of university training who could delegate therapeutic analyses to "auxiliaries", adherents of lay analysis with medical cover, and adherents of the integration of Freudianism with psychology under the category of "clinical psychology". The heterodox practice of Lacan, the measured use of variable length and shorter sessions, had been the object of debate in the SPP twice; it could draw on the rule of 1949 which stated that the "movement" of the training analysis "frequency, length, indeed suspension of sessions—remains as subject to the details of the particular case as a therapeutic analysis" (Art. V). Against this background of institutional conflict, Lacan's practice was again contested in the Administrative Council of the Institute in February 1953: Daniel Lagache upheld the right to experimentation and research, Nacht excluded this right from the training, putting in question the admission of the candidates in analysis with Lacan, while the latter justified his practice in terms of his clinical experience. The logic of the three arguments was in agreement with the positions taken by these three analysts in relation to the current conflict, positions which bore on the institution of training and hence the manner of tying analytical experience to institutional politics.

In 1952, when the SPP planned to reopen an institute charged with the task of organizing theoretical and practical teaching, Balint and Sachs had already stigmatized the impasses of the IPA training; Balint's text had been circulated in the SPP on Lacan's initiative. Bernfeld's lecture was contemporary with the French crisis and had not yet been published; Freud's judgement on the "juvenile shortcomings" of the institutes was either ignored (the postscript of 1927e was untranslated) or minimized or misunderstood. The initial project provided for the SPP to keep the prerogative of training analyses by co-opting the training analysts, and the Teaching Committee had the task of doctrine, regulation, selection, and admission conferred by the 1949 rules. The statutes that Nacht, as President of the SPP, proposed for this second association, the Institute, were received by the liberals like a *coup d'état*. Not only did he conflate his function as president with that of director of both associations and apportion himself a major part of the teaching while putting the seminars of Lacan and Lagache in competition on the same timetable, but he also undid the complex equilibrium between the three agencies by giving the Institute jurisdiction over the Committee while reducing the SPP to a "learned society". He effected the very separation between research and training so feared by Freud and condemned by Sachs.

The crisis then about to unfold for a year played on two levels which were fated to cross each other: power and the politics of analysis. Issues of power opposed the liberals, grouped around Lagache, to the autocratic ambitions of Nacht: very quickly the issue crystallized around a possible split, first brandished as a threat by Nacht, then acted on in the end by Lagache, who misunderstood its consequences; the discord partially overlapped an opposition between a medical and an academic psychological orientation; alliance and counter-alliance came to be decisive. The other issue of psychoanalytic politics was articulated by Lacan, who refused the logic of splitting and did not recognize himself in the two factions; he worked instead to amend the statutes of Nacht (Miller, 1976, pp. 52–63). It was a project that merits study because it anticipates Lacan's future institutional innovation, and it helps us to understand the distance between the two.

Sachs had understood his nomination as trainer in Berlin, while a member of the Vienna Psychoanalytic Society, as an attempt to separate the political responsibilities in the group from its didactic task; Bernfeld confirmed that Sachs held fast to this separation. Yet his case remained isolated, the confusion between the agencies of power and analytic responsibility being the rule. Against this confusion in one place of doctrinal authority and political power, Lacan promoted in his project "a unity of authority" (the administrative council) which respected a separation of doctrinal and political functions (Art. VI). To this end, he re-established the autonomy of the Teaching Commission, restoring to it its function of regulation and doctrine, dividing between it and the Management Committee of the Institute the responsibilities around seminars and courses; he established the rule according to which one could not be at the same time secretary of the Institute and member of the Commission; he instituted the recognition of an analytical *gradus*, which pertained to "the order of transmission of experience from the qualified analyst to candidate psychoanalyst". This "gradus", sanctioned by the title "certified by the Institute", was to familiarize the candidate with the practice of analysis, subject to the legal requirements of the exercise of medicine; it was therefore distinct from the title of "adherent" of the SPP which had been until then the only title to indicate one had completed the *cursus*, and which perpetuated the hierarchy between adherent and titular trainer. The project proposed a second title (Assistant at the Institute) conferred for "eminent collaboration" in the work of the Institute without qualifying for practice; the teachings were not to be reserved solely for aspiring analysts.

In re-establishing the Commission's responsibility in the transmission of experience, this project aimed to counter the danger of personal politics of the Management Committee and the confusion of agencies. However, it also had the ambition to counter the formalization of studies, its exigencies of assiduousness and the rigid temporality of its prescribed *cursus*, with a principle of "liberally conceived" study, a principle required by a "humanist" science and by the necessity of a student acquiring a discipline by means of real participation in the "research that founds the categories of analytic experience". If the necessity to open an institute is clearly linked by Lacan to the duty to distinguish the principles of analytic discipline from the psychotherapies at a time when these latter "reach the level of social phenomena", the teaching programme is explicitly linked to the "fantastical" idea of Freud of a Higher School (Hauté École) of analysis. (It is amusing to highlight the chiasmus operated by the translation used (from German to French): the *Hochschule* becomes a "Faculty" (Faculté) and the *Falkultät* becomes a "School" (École); the return of the term School for a psychoanalytic institution will take place with the naming of the École Freudienne de Paris.)

This passage about the *Hochschule* from *The Question of Lay Analysis* was placed as an epigraph to the passage outlining the content. Four permanent seminars were proposed: the textual seminars, the oral commentary of an original text being "the surest and most rational means of methodical access to the fundamental concepts of analysis" while preserving a "living tradition"; the supervised study of technique in which "the creative function of praxis" can be recognized, "the relation of rules to their effects in a case" being the way of the "science of the particular"; a seminar of clinical and phenomenological criticism aiming to question classical psychopathology and its effective value in clinical intervention; lastly, a seminar on child analysis. Special seminars would then allow the Institute to end the doctrinal isolation of analysis and to fulfil its task as "designated host for dialogue with related disciplines". Besides this first "office" of higher teaching and research, a second office of the institute would allow for "internships" (clinic of neuroses, techniques for their treatment, symptoms and contraindications) and a model dispensary annexed to a hospital.

The primacy given to speech in the teaching suggests that its effects on a listener would produce, "even silently", a "dialogue" which presented a symmetry with the experience of a training analysis. Lacan held that this symmetry, touched the heart of the problem that "the place of analysis in the system of sciences" represented, and that it was required by the specificity of analysis in relation to what it received from closely related sciences and what it gave them. He was thus trying to activate a knot between knowledge and experience that had already inspired the text of 1949. This path of "dialogue" echoed the rhetorical device Freud had chosen to transmit to his interlocutor the scandal of lay analysis.

Like Freud, Lacan might have hoped that his project would be agreed upon rather than compromised, in so far as he anticipated unity from a dismembered body by offering it the "instrument of a mirror" that gave the *reason* for division: a reason to be found in the original "Discord", to which the second Topography "gave another name" (Lacan, 1976, p. 52). Doubtless, Lacan believed in it more than Freud, who ended his dialogue on a disagreement; his letter to Loewenstein bears witness to the months of despair and nightmare that followed. As well as betrayals of friendship and the "group effects" involving those very people who had known the Occupation, there was a style, and forms of human relationship, analogous to those of the Terror or the Prague trials (Lacan, 1976, pp. 120–135).

In effect, issues of power had gained the upper hand over the project of setting up a training faithful to analytic particularity; the play of alliances and compromises had won over the agreement Lacan hoped for, repressing, but not for long, discord, and allowing the opening of an institute that conformed to Nacht's vision. The latter then took a symptomatic decision that would put the French style *gentleman's agreement* to the test and turn the discord into a split. When, in May 1953, the analysts in training received a form which asked them to renew their commitment not to take on the title of analyst and not to practise without authorization from the Committee, they were very upset. Was the new form a way of annulling their training until then? While the analysts in training had not thought of questioning their commitment as such, the symptomatic dimension of this event brought to the fore the confusion with respect to authority. Nacht told Jenny Roudinesco heavy-handedly that she was in error by jointly addressing the President of the Society, Lacan, and the Director of the Institute, Nacht, when the latter alone was in charge of the administration. It was likely that her letter revoked the separation Nacht had introduced, but it was also underestimating the fact that she was addressing the two analysts to whom she owed her training, her didactician and one of her two supervisors, in order to convey the malaise of the students and how it was wrong to treat them as minors and pupils (Miller, 1976). Nacht's administrative blunder revealed his confiscation, for his own autocracy, of the Commission's authority and his wish to efface the training powers of the SPP. The support of the liberals for this revolt of the students could not but lead to a split.

Because this revolt erupted around the question of authorization, it brought back the question, not reducible to an opposition between liberalism and autocracy, of the authority in play in analysis and its institutions. Freud had emphasized that the analyst's authority derived from the transference and not from any diploma or guarantee attaching to a training, even a medical one. But what is its foundation? Is it subject to transmission, whether apostolic, by investiture, filiation, or initiation? Does it require a place, and which one, in the institution? Lacan was going to become the addressee of this question, which, at that date, could not be heard better in Paris than in London, where, ironic coincidence, the first IPA conference devoted to training was at last going to be held, in July 1953.

Letter of Jenny Roudinesco, 15 May 1953

To Dr Nacht, Director of the Institute of Psychoanalysis and to Dr Lacan, President of the Society of Psychoanalysis

Dear Friends

Some days ago I received a circular concerning decisions of the Teaching Committee with a promise to be signed which, to be honest, has thrown me into confusion. First of all the respective roles of the Society and the Institute are not clear and hence I am addressing the Director of the one and the President of the other, since I am in any case linked to both by ties of friendship and recognition for their help in my analytic training.

I first asked to commence a training analysis in April 1949 when only the Society existed and at that time the Committee of seven people gave its agreement. I then took the oath on my honour not to practise analysis without authorisation and not to authorise myself with the title of analyst before being elected member of the Society. This oath was not unilateral as the Committee and Society on their part were morally committed to confer my title when I had satisfied the demands of my analyst, my supervisors and received the accreditation of the Society on the Committee's recommendation.

Now I am being asked for a new oath whose necessity I fail to understand and which I can only take if I know its cause as with the first oath. What preoccupies me is ignorance on the one hand of any new statutes in the Institute and Society, and on the other hand, the terms used to communicate the decisions of the Training Committee which seem to imply a retroactive effect for these decisions. I am perfectly aware of the resistances encountered by analysis and of the work we desire to pursue in common, as well as the necessity of arming ourselves with all the moral and professional guarantees before we confer the title of analyst and the responsibilities they entail, yet these difficulties should not provoke a feeling of insecurity among analysts, pushing them to an autocratic attitude incompatible with the very nature of the work undertaken.

As it happens my personal situation is not in question. I started my analysis because I realised it was impossible to conduct psychotherapies of children correctly without knowing the analytic discipline; it allowed me, without being the easiest way given my age and situation, to resolve my personal problems to my and your satisfaction; one of my supervisions with Lebovici has been completed with his approval since April, the other is ongoing, but with your approval I intended to submit my essay and apply for membership with the Society very shortly.

As you would know from my analysis, dear M. Nacht, I consider myself, I believe legitimately, to have been associated for a while already with the common work of spreading analytic thought.

I have proved myself as an organiser and as a team head, I have teaching experience and some knowledge of group reactions. That is why I allow myself to tell you that there is malaise among the young candidates for analysis and in my opinion this malaise can only be lifted if the Society communicated statutes and internal rules, so they can be studied and criticisms and opinions formulated in all liberty.

A large number of them have reached a full maturity and flowering of their personality precisely because of analysis and they would only suffer in being treated as minors and pupils.

I therefore ask you to take my letter into consideration and communicate it to the Society and the Administrative Council of the Institute for discussion.

Please believe, dear friends, in my complete devotion to the common cause.

Jenny Roudinesco

Notes

1. In his talks at Saint-Anne in 1972, Lacan interpreted the control of psychoanalysis by medicine as an effect of the fact that its relations "with the discourse of science were becoming increasingly narrow" (seminar of 1 June 1972).
2. In 1978, Lacan would say that "of course, this *pass* is a complete failure". Thus, we introduce a question of the logic shared by these two failures.

CHAPTER FOUR

From one Training to Another

A professional training?

During the inauguration of the Institute of Psychoanalysis in June 1954, a year after the split, the Minister for National Education emphasized, in the presence of the Minister for Health, that the teachings and training planned for the Institute already existed at university level, and that it was important to set up a collaboration between psychologists and doctors to establish "a science of man" (Miller, 1976, pp. 156–157). While expressing the wish to remain outside of the polemics dividing analysts, he gave his support to the founders of the French Society of Psychoanalysis (SFP). The editorial board of the *Revue française de psychanalyse*, which published the speech, made it clear in a footnote that only the Institute was recognized by the IPA as a teaching body; in 1955, the Central Executive rejected once again the request for affiliation by the "Lagache group" because of their "lack of training capacity".

These inaugural statements need to be emphasized because, in his statutes of 1952, Nacht already planned a diploma which he hoped the state would recognize. In his presentation, he insisted on the medical roots of analysis, distancing himself from "Freud's old dream", that is, the "fantastical idea" of 1926: "we will take care for our part not to aim that high". He favoured instead the experimental medicine of Claude Bernard as a reference point for the teaching of analytic technique. Some weeks after the split, Lacan had written to his analyst, Loewenstein, to describe the "extravagant" events of the previous months, communicate his regret that the "medical core" had crystallized around Nacht, hostile to lay analysis, and to assure him that the new "work community" is not the "clan of psychologists" they were made out to be (Miller, 1976, pp 120–135). This shows the singularity of his position, which made of him the sticking point in the SFP's negotiation to reintegrating the IPA, and determined him, also in the question of training, to stage a "return to Freud". Before exploring its movement and history, it is important to understand the social moment in which the question of the training of analysts was inscribed.

Beyond the conflict between autocracy and liberalism, which did not lead to a decisive split, Nacht and Lagache shared a common preoccupation, in conformity with the one orientating the IPA since the inception in 1925 of the International Training Committee: organizing the professional training of analysts. It was an orientation that was in line, intentionallly or not, with the process of rationalization in Western society analysed by Max Weber and of which the slow substitution of professions for the arts, crafts, and other activities was a major part. In this process, the institutionalization of professional training was crucial. By downgrading the initiatory or speculative modes of transmission, it contributed to the transformation of those practices and their social status. A precondition for this was the formalization of knowledge, particularly of technical knowledge or know-how. This latter was long excluded from the university, despite the fact that universities also trained for "professions" such as theologian and jurist; it was recognized in its specificity by the encyclopaedists and the setting up, in France, of the "Grandes Écoles". This recognition, as well as the organization of its transmission, were side effects of the reciprocal link between modern science and modern technology, a reciprocity which is at work in the rendering of physics more mathematical and instrumental, and which breaks with the ancient way of positioning oneself in relation to the objects of knowledge and technical objects. The question of training, and the rationalization of the profession it was meant to effect, thus became a crucial component in the strategies of social recognition, identification, organization of a profession, and even its legitimacy.

Did Freud invent a new profession when he invented a new social bond? We have seen that this was at the heart of the debate of 1927 on lay analysis, more for Jones, who recoiled from the idea of an independent profession, than for Freud, who did not formulate this. When he proposed, in 1919, the project of teaching analysis at university (for the training of doctors and not analysts, who, to him, had already found their proper place and modality), he dreamt of the possibility of linking medicine to the teachings grouped under philosophy. He dreamt of this again in 1926 with respect to the training of analysts. Should one take his reference to the *universitas literarum* and his belief in the power of "letters" as a foundation for the universality of knowledge as sheer archaism? It is important to grasp the link between this reference and Freud's resistance to those processes of which the movement of professionalization forms a part, processes which intimately link modern science, technology, and capitalist markets. Is it the same logic that led Freud to call upon the *universitas literarum* and to oppose the decision of his American colleagues, judging that their decision to proscribe the practice of analysis to lay people, whatever the social, economic, or political motives, was an attempt to repress analysis (Freud, 1926e, pp. 251–258, pages not published by Jones and Eitingon)? How should one understand this position in relation to the scientific requirements of analysis? Freud's reserve regarding the attempt at professionalization sheds light on the recurrent attempt—temptation?—on the part of analysts to situate their practice within an existing profession (medicine) or one on its way to becoming one (psychotherapy) and to refer, for its transmission, to a similarity with a trade. One of the reasons for this temptation relates to the difficulty of maintaining a social bond for which the categories of trade and profession are inadequate, and which Lacan would develop with the writing of his "discourses".

Subject to all the ideological, economic, and social pressures that control of a profession brings, professional training was developed in the twentieth century, seeking to distinguish itself from teaching, learning, and education, but keeping a link to each. It was an attempt to respond to social pressures to co-ordinate scientific, technological, and economic variables. It put into play different modes of articulation and emphasis concerning the acquisition of knowledge and know-how, aims of adaptation, and of transformation of the person. A dominant logic of training would emerge depending on whether what was privileged was the subject's relation to knowledge, to society, or the relation of knowledge to the profession (Fabre, 1994). Variants of this logic will depend on the choice to emphasize the structure or the acquisition of knowledge, its systematic dimension, or the register of problems, the technical side of methods and mechanisms, or skill and intuition. The rhetoric of the discourse of training often takes up a way of thinking change, inherited from Aristotle: notions of transmission, quantity, quality, structure of knowledge, all occur in the schemas of his *Physics*. Likewise, the dominant model of training, the "one forms", posits the passage from some initial state to a final state according to the paradigm of an artisanal craft and following a distribution of causality set up by the same tradition: the material with which an object is to be made, the form given to it, the end determining this form, and the agency necessary to produce the effect.

Modern science, in instrumentalizing and mathematizing physics, had to break with a physics dealing with real beings, empirical and subject to changes according to Aristotelian causality and its schemas, as it had to make literal a demonstrative mathematics tied to the necessary, the eternal and the immobile. The reference to the artisanal model in the training of analysts, whether explicit or not, does not take this break into account, yet it privileges a reification of the individual to be trained which may seem to conform to scientific and technical objectivity. In preferring the workshop of the master craftsman to the laboratory in training the analyst, as in "the noble crafts of yore", Eitingon followed the principle of "one trains". It can, in fact, seem consistent, even commonsensical, that with respect to a therapeutic end of analytic practice, the doctor to whom a trainer gives the form of analyst (his own: his own knowledge, his own technique, his own ego) is, usually, the only suitable material. In orientating itself thus, the IPA training organization did not take into account the unconscious determination of the subject's relation to knowledge, the dimension of experience, and not experimentation, in the treatment, nor did it question the participation of analysis in the social phenomenon of psychotherapies and the effect of this participation on its own doctrine.

In accordance with a pedagogic discourse critical of technological and institutional rationality, Bernfeld proposed to organize training according to the contested logic of "training oneself". This critical position that a model conceived for beings who derive their form from something other than themselves has value for beings who have the potential for change within themselves. It emphasizes the register of experience, taken as the privileged place of training to the point of being identical to it. The tradition of the *Bildungsroman* had developed the process by means of which an individual acquires his form. It is his own form to start with, but grasped in the movement in which, through a personal myth or work, following chance encounters, it realizes itself; it takes on meaning and truth in its retroactive decipherment. The social aim is less adaptation than integration into a community through a process of universalization of the particular form, which is not received from the other, even if it is the occasion of its realization. It is the *Phenomenology of Spirit*, as "science of experience and consciousness", which is its most accomplished philosophical expression; it has the ambition of passing from love of knowledge to "effectively real knowledge", that is, to "the scientific system" of truth (Hegel, 1979). To effect this passage is, according to Hegel, to apprehend the truth, not as substance but as subject, in its movement of positing itself by means of its own becoming other; it is recognizing the subject as pure negativity and division. Experience is "the dialectical movement that consciousness operates in itself, in its knowledge as much as in its object". This movement of auto-formation, which has "at first its own end as aim", necessitates "enduring the length of the process", of "dwelling" at each moment with the same patience that the "spirit of the world" did in undertaking the prodigious work of universal history. Work, in which the master–slave dialectic is played out, and action, in which finite particularity is accepted and where the movement of work takes place, are the paths of a training which finds its full meaning, with language, in the moment of culture.

Lacan always emphasized the dimension of experience of analysis. Already, in 1936, he defined this latter as an experience of language in which the space created by Freud for the testimony of the subject, in order to access the real that the treatment is working to transform, renews the alliance of science and truth. Specifying in 1951 that "analysis is a dialectical experience", he found in Hegel a support for his development of the "progress of the subject" in the treatment (Lacan, 2006a). Even though this development applies to the "training experience" that the analysis of the analyst is, it situates it rather differently than the technological paradigm guiding the training model of the IPA. In the pages in which Lacan analysed the "series of dialectical reversals" with which Freud presented the case of Dora, giving to the reader "the scansion of the structures in which truth is transmuted for the subject", he denounced the new form of alienation of man in which analysis risked participating. Taking refuge in psychologism out of fear of the truth spoken by the "illnesses that speak", were the practitioners who perpetuated analytic technique going to let themselves be hypnotized by the fabrication of a *homo psychologicus* and contribute to the selection of "techniques having the training scope of rites", or were they going to maintain the "salutary value" of Freud's initiative (*ibid.*, pp. 177–178)? In order to grasp the scope of his criticism, it is important to emphasize that, at the same time, Lacan held that technique organizes experience as much as the system of concepts, and that "technical training commands theoretical intelligence itself". In denouncing the danger menacing analysis, he appealed to experience in order to save the technique that founds Freudian experience in its rigour from the technological ritualization in which it was losing itself; this at the very moment in which his colleagues summoned him to explain the gap between the length of his sessions and the ritual duration required by the standard treatment.

The question of technique

A crisis shook the Secret Committee in 1924, leading to its (temporary) dissolution by Freud. It crystallized around the modifications of "classical technique" envisaged by Ferenczi and Rank, but it was the latter's theoretical construction that, above all, alarmed Jones and Abraham (Ferenczi & Rank, 1956; Rank, 1929). By systematically experimenting with a fixed end date to analysis, Rank had encountered clinical effects that he sought to elaborate with the notion of "birth trauma". Abraham considered his theory a scientific regression in which "repetition of the Jung case" was being played out; Freud, in a letter to the Committee dated 15 February 1924, countered this alarming and hurtful rejection with an open and prudent position (Jones, 1957, pp. 62–65). Even if Ferenczi's "active therapy" advocated in Budapest in 1919, represented "a dangerous temptation for ambitious beginners" in his eyes, Freud recognized that the common work of Ferenczi and Rank brought an extension and a correction to his concepts of repetition and *agieren* which were worthy of further reflection. "We must guard ourselves against straightaway dismissing such an enterprise as heretical". In giving their due to the secondary tendencies which, in all scientific work, push in the direction of finding new and surprising things, he took the theoretical question posed by Rank very seriously. He, who was normally so unattuned to the thought of others that he could not even censor it, undertook to examine the contradictions that Rank brought to his own theory of Oedipus, incest taboo, and paternal function. That analysis, beyond the crisis, would contribute to the reordering, a year later, of the relation between anxiety and repression; and it was involved in the development of the notion of fetishism in which Freud found confirmation of the primacy of castration anxiety. While conveying his doubts about the possibility of shortening analyses, Freud concluded his letter to the Committee thus: "I will wait for the day a sustained reflection and experimentation result in a clarification". At the same time, he tried to make Abraham understand that the risk of error, hard to avoid in scientific work, does not prevent one living under the same roof during the time it takes to evaluate a discovery and the technical modifications it entails; and he also discussed closely with Ferenczi and Rank his own position, more and more reserved, with respect to the latter's book.

The *Encyclopédie médico-chirurgicale*, which, at Henri Ey's request, included in 1955 the articles of Maurice Bouvet, "La cure-type", and of Lacan, "Variantes de la cure-type", was a catch-all fiction. With his seminar of 1953–1954 on Freud's technical writings, the *Rome Discourse*, as well as *Variantes de la cure-type*, Lacan was holding up for public inspection the question of technique, its theoretical importance, its scientific and social co-ordinates, and its implications for the training of analysts. His *Encyclopaedia* article went on the offensive by denouncing the deviations from so-called "classical" technique and the theoretical misunderstandings they derived from (Lacan, 2006b). By linking a diachronic and synchronic approach, he situated around 1920 the moment in which technique, with the analysis of "material" and the analysis of resistances, ensnared itself in the lures of the ego. Where the very term "material" discredits "psychoanalytic semantics", that is, the discourse of the unconscious, the attribution of resistance to the ego at the very moment that Freud uncovered the resistances of id and superego engaged theory and technique in a contradiction. "The constituting subject of the symptom is treated as already constituted" and the ego constituted in resistance is treated as the constituting agency to which the analyst addresses himself—as an ego himself. This is misrecognizing what is taught by analytic technique: the speech it reveals is the stuff of an unconscious subject. This misrecognition is closure of the unconscious; it is fleeing from the action required of the analyst when he has consented to deliver speech, which is an act implying a subject. No doubt one has to recognize in this fleeing "the fear taking hold of one when uncovering the shape of one's power" in the act in which it shows itself "naked"; yet, this is how it shows itself in "each experience humbly led by one of the workers trained [in Freud's school]" (Lacan, 2006c, p. 201). The difficulties of the countertransference are a shelter for this fear; the malaise in the training must be understood as the "rebellion of the facts" against this closure of the unconscious and misrecognition of the truth.

Lacan did not speak in this article of the technical variation that he was criticized for and on which he was questioned. Instead, he rejected the notion of standard treatment by recalling Freud's reservations with respect to standardizing a technique which was appropriate first of all to his own personality. In the *Rome Discourse*, he explained the clinical reasons for manipulating the length of the session; he differentiated it from the active technique of setting a fixed end; he held that the time needed for the unconscious to reveal itself did not derive from "timing", but from the time of the subject in speech as well as "the time to create a symbolic object" (*ibid.*, pp. 255–257). The temporal dialectic of logical time and the practice of punctuation in constructing a text, give better access to it than the modern technical object that is the clock of Huyghens.

Lacan also gave, in the preface to the *Rome Discourse*, a reading of the temporality in which that paper was inscribed. It "takes its meaning and form" from the haste received from the circumstances, that is, the split that had just taken place. He related his decision to leave the SPP, together with the founders of the SFP, to that moment when a man "can identify in a single reason the side he takes and the disorder he denounces, in order to understand their coherence in the real and anticipate by his certainty the action that weighs them against each other" (*ibid.*, p. 201). His choice is thus read, retroactively, as issuing from a moment of understanding. "An overtaking in speech" of this haste, the July lecture, "The Symbolic, the Imaginary and the Real" and the *Rome Discourse* show, with this institutional conflict re training, how Lacan came out of a period of theoretical development, the end of a long road which was necessary to go beyond the exploration of the specular imaginary and the resistances of the ego. The handling of time which was a stumbling block for his colleagues became the new cornerstone, on which he would not compromise. His clinical, technical, and theoretical approach to time did indeed play a major role in this displacement.

In his thesis of 1932, Lacan noted that, according to the masters themselves, the technique for dealing with psychoses was not yet ripe and this was "the most burning problem of analysis" (Lacan, 1975b, pp. 279–280), "for a stagnation of technical results at their current level would quickly lead to the degradation of doctrine" (*ibid.*, pp. 313–314). The two thorny problems were the transference, in relation to the problem of the triggering of psychosis, and the resistances, due to the integration of the analyst's interpretations into the delusion. Of the three poles he used in order to capture the phenomenon of personality (individual, structural, and social), it was the last which seemed to him most propitious to a scientific approach, even when aiming at the other two. Thus, he came to write that the therapeutic problem of psychoses renders "a psychoanalysis of the ego more necessary than an analysis of the unconscious" and that the study of resistances and "a new experience of their handling" would furnish "the foundations of a new analytic technique". In 1936 he presented, with the mirror stage, the theory of a "structuring moment" in the constitution of reality, and he specified what the consequence would be for analytic technique: to fix the times of operation of analysis in the two registers of interpretation and transference, depending on the reactions of the subject (Lacan, 2006d, p. 68). While pursuing the investigation of imaginary identification with which he developed the social side, Lacan was exploring the handling of resistance by means of handling time: for, in neurosis also, the material produced in the treatment can come to satisfy the resistance. He saw in this one of the motifs which led Freud, in 1918, to support Ferenczi's active technique (Freud, 1919a, p. 162). Lacan wanted to "disconcert" those cases, especially in obsessional neurosis and in training analyses, in which the ritual application to work reinforces resistance. In doing so, he was applying to the length of the session the technical ideas of Freud concerning the "right moment", themselves derived from the moral and political tradition of reflection on the *kairos*.

With the invention in 1945 of the temporal dialectic of logical time, Lacan could tie together the three poles (individual, social, and structural) at the basis of an understanding of psychosis and it gave the theoretical foundation for the handling of time (Lacan, 2006e). But it also answered the question of 1936: "How does the 'I' in which the subject recognizes itself constitute itself amongst its typical identifications?" Using the terms of this temporality, Lacan could redevelop the mirror stage as "constitutive of the function of the 'I'", as manifesting "the symbolic matrix in which the 'I' is precipitated in a primordial form, prior to being objectified in the dialectic of identification with the other, and before language restores to it, in the universal, its function as subject" (Lacan, 2006f, p. 76). In this way "logical time" allowed Lacan to pass from the first triad of the 1932 thesis to the triad Symbolic, Imaginary and Real. By knotting the Symbolic and the Imaginary, the text allowed one to distinguish them, and even, according to Lacan in 15 June 1955, it was expressly done with this intention; it also allowed, with the "proper link of a human being to the time that is haste", to knot together speech, the act, and truth. One can then perhaps see why Lacan never compromised on the technique founded by this development and why a rereading and even rewriting of "Logical Time" always remained on his agenda (Porge, 1989).

The sophism of the prisoners in "Logical Time" allows us to shed light on something of the context of the question of technique, which was decisive beyond the field of technique itself. The text was looking for "the logical form of all 'human' assimilation" in so far as it presents itself as "assimilating a barbarism". Lacan entrusted it to a magazine, *Les Cahiers d'Art*, which carried the dates 1940–1944 in parentheses on its cover. In 1946, during the psychiatric congress at Bonneval, he confessed to having had the fantasy of his hand being full of truths in order the better to hold onto them; he recognized in this "a failure on my part to live up to what the course of the world demands of me" in those years of "humiliation of our times, faced with the enemies of human kind" (Lacan, 2006g, p. 123). The movement which, in the 1950s, brought Lacan to rethink the conditions and ends of the training of analysts was inseparable from three factors: his questioning of the "modern technicians" of analysis who barricaded themselves behind the primacy of technique without re-evaluating its foundation, restoring the truth of the experience which the new technique misrecognized; and the task of formalization, by means of which analysis can hold its place and responsibility among the sciences and in relation to modern subjectivity. We ventured the hypothesis that the initiative to institute a professional training of analysts was determined by certain effects of the First World War, and it seems to us equally necessary to recognize that Lacan was determined, in his own approach to these questions, by the specifics of the second. The cornerstone allowing him to introduce the heteronomy of the Symbolic was the concept of "logical time", which also involved a dimension of the act. It is the index of the place reserved in Lacan's development for the worst event of the century; it anticipated his manner of articulating and constructing a question that insists: can psychoanalysis orientate itself, in its clinic, its theory, and its collectivity, on the real of structure stripped bare by the Shoah (Brainin & Kaminer, 1982; Stern, 1998)?

Lacan's paradoxical position towards technique and science is related to this question. To save technique from technicality and to save science from positivism is not possible without questioning their "intersection" with modern forms of eugenics and the "brazen face of capitalist exploitation". In the *Rome Discourse*, Lacan distinguished and put into a series three paradoxical relations of speech to language in the subject that the analyst encounters in his field: the neurotic economy of symptom, inhibition, and anxiety, the alienation of madness, and the alienation of the "subject of scientific civilisation" (Lacan, 2006c, pp. 232–233). He emphasized the closeness of the last two alienations and "formidable responsibility" of the analyst when, with a manipulation of doctrine, he provides a supplementary occasion for alienation in the ego. He correlated the risk taken in promoting the ego both to the free enterprise of which it is the "theology", and to a "technological enterprise at a planetary level". In situating man as an individual, reducible to a biological individual, liberated certainly, yet doomed to a "social misery", the promotion of the ego paradoxically brings modern man closer to the "original rending" that Freud had formulated with his death drive, ever more menaced by the objectivation pursued by scientific technique (Lacan, 2006b, p. 279; 2006g, p. 156). This notion of an alienation specific to the subject of scientific civilization is a reworking in 1953 of a concern Lacan had in the years following the war. It offers a perspective on a discontent in civilization which does not strictly follow the Freudian version if one ventures the hypothesis that the three paradoxical relations of speech and language in neurosis, madness, and scientific civilization can be related to the three modes of negation in which truth makes itself heard (repression, foreclosure, and denial). It means that, for Lacan, the social bond is not a question of professional recognition (a version of adaptation for the analyst), but a question posed to the analyst in his clinic, his theory, his technique, and his own way of making a collective. If it behoves the analyst to rejoin the subjectivity of his time, the horizon of the "real, all too real fact" of the concentration camps becomes, like time, a cornerstone.

These co-ordinates that he gave to the question of technique also explain his closeness to, and distance from, the question that Heidegger constructed, through language, in order to found on the unveiling of the truth of technique a free relation to it. The objective of his 1953 lecture was to grasp, in the very place of the "monstrous element" which makes modern technique the greatest danger, what can save one from that danger (Heidegger, 1977). He undid the apparent opposition between *technè*, in the sense of artisanal making, and the *phusis*, in the sense of the flower coming into being without passing through artist or artisan. These two modalities, which found the antithetical paradigms of the discourses of training, were subsumed under the category of *poiêsis*, production, which itself partook of the movement of unveiling of truth (*alêtheia*). The four modalities of the *aition*, from which philosophical discourse forged the four "causes", are as valid for nature as for a profession. Heidegger followed the same path in order to subsume under the category of "destiny of unveiling", "given" to man, the ancient mode of *poiêsis* and the modern one of "enframing" (*Gestell*), in which man, in a process of accumulation, is "provoked" into "putting forward the real as stock" (*Bestand*). Against the commonplace notion that modern technology is an application, abusive in the long term, of science, he put forward the notion that modern physics, in which nature is "summoned" to answer as calculable system of data, already obeys, before the slightest application, the mode of enframing. The ambiguity of the essence of technique, of that destiny of unveiling which can bring man to guard the truth or to veil it by entering into "the furious movement of securing", derives from the ambiguity inherent in the very movement of unveiling and obscuring the truth. Meditation, questioning, "piety of thought", in finding again the "poetic thing" that was the proper name of unveiling, can save one from the danger that the very ambiguity of truth brings with it.

The essence of Lacan's development of the question of technique in analytic practice was already completed when Heidegger's lecture was published and translated. Keeping in mind the Heideggerian accents of the first reference to truth in order to think the Symbolic, it is no surprise that Heidegger's meditation is very close to the reformulation Lacan made of analytic technique as "technique of speech". If this expression, which corrected the "art of speech" of 1956, is right, it is not only because of the fundamental rule proposed to the analysand, but also because the analyst both "delivers" this speech, and plays with the power of resonance of words while punctuating the text of the analysand so as to fix its meaning. To learn and teach this technique requires "the profound assimilation of the resources of a language", particularly those realized in its poetry, notably in "the poetics of the Freudian oeuvre". Yet, there remains an essential distance between Lacan and Heidegger. The latter does not really elaborate on the risk that man, committed to unveiling "the real as capital", would consider "human material" itself as capital. In appropriating the word *Gestell* to signify this operation, he did not fail to note that this term he posited (*Stell, stellen*) was as valid for describing police methods of interpellation (stopping someone in the street and interrogating them) as for the workings of science in accounting for things (Heidegger, 1977, pp. 26–29). Lacan, for his part, denounced the technique of "human engineering"; he recalled the "Swiftian humour" of Georges Canguilhem on this issue (Canguilhem, 1968; Lacan, 2006h, p. 730). He did not seek to subsume these modes of enframing under some essence of technique. In this sense, the question of technique rather brought out the tension between the scientific requirement for formalization of knowledge and the requirements of truth.

This tension might account for one aspect of both the conflict with the IPA around technique and the new split provoked by the scrapping of Lacan from the list of trainers. At the same time as his technique, intolerable to the orthopraxis of the IPA, something from his theoretical development was also rejected. This had less to do with his work on the subject of the signifier, which was perhaps tolerable because it allowed doctrinal pluralism, than with his position with respect to truth. Something can be gleaned from the suspicion cast by the "modern technicians" of the IPA on Lacan's charisma and his position as master. For his part, Lacan accused them of failing to "consider the action incumbent [to the analyst] in the production of truth" (Lacan, 2006b, p. 276) because of a ritualized technicalism and its theoretical confusions (specifically concerning countertransference and interpretation). He could write that by punctuating the dialectic at work in the speech of the analysand, the analyst was "the master of the truth, of which this discourse constitutes the progress".

Did Lacan revive one of the figures of "masters of truth" from the prehistory of Parmenides (Detienne, 1999) when he inscribed technique in the register of *poiêsis*? The stress put on the handling of the "poetic function of language" and on the "oracular side" of interpretation evokes the powers of speech with respect to truth, of the poet, diviner, and the king of justice, from a time before the secularization of speech replaced them, not without a remainder, with a philosophical reflection on *logos* and *alêtheia*. At the very moment that Lacan started the formalization which would allow him to undo the "collusion" between the analyst and the truth and his confusion with the Other, the IPA was tightening its evaluation of technique in an inquisitorial way (Roudinesco, 1990, pp. 318–369). In August 1961, the *ad hoc* Committee appointed to investigate the position of the SFP formulated the Edinburgh 'Recommendations' aimed at its members, with a view to standardizing training and excluding Lacan and Dolto (see *L'Excommunication*, Miller, 1977a, p. 19). The fascination with a fantasized master of truth, at play during the enquiry, and the final rejection of Lacan, contributed to fixate more than one of them in the same fascination for the doings, gestures, and words of Lacan.

The development of the theory of *das Ding* allowed Lacan to substitute the idea of creation (... and training) for the artisanal imagery inherited from Aristotle, a process of creation in which the secular vase of the potter, taken up by Heidegger in his text, is to be understood as "an object made to represent the existence of the void at the heart of the real called the Thing" (Lacan, 1999, pp. 121–122). The potter, like the analyst, "creates the vase around this emptiness with his hand"; the vase is "a fashioned signifier". This void should be added to the four causes of the technological model. In the same year, while working on his "Remark on the rapport of Daniel Lagache", Lacan could close the period he had needed to "sweep away the imaginary that was too stuck in technique": "We are no longer at that stage". The term technique would rarely appear in his writings after that. The rewriting of a passage of "Variations on the standard treatment" confirmed that the question of the ethics of discourse had replaced the question of technique. For "respect for certain forms of technique, recognised as essential by all analysts beyond variations in the treatment" of the first edition, he substituted in 1966 "the rigour that is in some sense ethical" and the requirement of a formalization rather than a practical formalism (Lacan, 2006b, pp. 269–270). Yet Lacan still had to elaborate a certain downgrading of truth while distinguishing its different determinations in order to articulate how analytic discourse was linked to it (Balmès, 1999). It is the seminar devoted to the four fundamental concepts that found analysis as praxis, after his exclusion, which allowed him to articulate two decisive ideas that would shift his position away from the response with which he confronted the technicism of the IPA from a position as a master of truth. The "power of the practitioner", which risks letting the "impossible" of analysis, according to Freud, be understood as impotence, made way for an exploration of the desire of the analyst. To the question posed in Rome in January 1964, during the Study Day organized by Enrico Castelli—"To what extent does the desire of the analyst bring analytic technique back to the world of techniques?"—Lacan answered, "These two things are heterogeneous" (Castelli, 1964; Lacan, 2006i). With the "subject supposed to know", the place of the analyst in the transference would be correlated to the supposition of a subject to unconscious knowledge and the object little *a*. That his truth as subject, even in the position of master, flared up for Lacan in the "negotiated" object that he was, was not unimportant to this shift (Lacan, 1991, p. 6).

The foundation of the school

In August of 1963, the IPA's Executive Committee excluded Lacan from training: "He is no longer recognized as a training analyst" (Miller, 1977a, p. 82). On 19 November 1963, the general assembly of the SFP confirmed this decision, as well as the measures concerning the analysands in training with him. The following day Lacan suspended, after a first and unique session, his seminar on the "Names of the Father". Two months later, "taken" in Section VI of the École Pratique des Hautes Études, he started a new seminar with the following questions: What joins and what separates analysis from science, religion, research, and alchemy? Which concepts (perhaps 'concepts in formation'?) anchor it as a *praxis*, that is, as an operation able to "treat the real by means of the symbolic"? (Lacan, 1991, p. 1–9). He mentions the "fact" of his exclusion at the start of his questions and interpreted it as a major excommunication, relating it to the *kherem* pronounced against Spinoza, to which he added the point of no return of a *shamta*. Lacan was forbidden to exercise his training function and his name had to be erased from the list of trainers. But he was not disqualified as analyst or forbidden from teaching. He was, therefore, not thrown out of the community of analysts, strictly speaking. Yet, he turned what would be a disciplinary prohibition in the church into something putting him beyond sacrament and ritual, and, in the case of the *kherem*, the prohibition of hearing and teaching Torah; a measure, therefore, which touched the essence of a subject's link to God and the community. What was the truth of this inexactitude, which would retroactively take on the dimension of a founding myth for him and his pupils?

Lacan "dedicated his life" to a teaching guided and determined by the training of analysts; his "return to Freud" was not just a formal operation, it was a real practice, inseparable from the practice of training. His distaste for the split of 1953 and his support for the negotiation for the affiliation of the SFP show the importance he attached to this practice being within the institution Freud had hoped would shelter analytic doctrine. In that practice, he renounced from the start, despite many misunderstandings, the differentiation between so-called therapeutic and training analyses, just as he did not accept the ruling forbidding analysands access to teaching. If the exclusion touched on his being as subject by making emerge, *après-coup*, the "negotiated" object he had been, it touched him also in his practice and his bonds with the community and tradition. If, from the point of view of the institutional split, it is inexact to speak of excommunication, it is truthful from the point of view of his real position and his practice.

During the unique session of the unpublished seminar "The Names of the Father", Lacan stressed, with the non-sacrifice of Isaac, "the cutting edge between God's enjoyment and what a certain tradition terms desire". He inscribed this non-seminar in the same tradition. By means of the *kherem* Spinoza was rejected from this tradition; like other heretics (their *pertinacia* bears witness to it) he wanted this separation in some way; he was not a founder and did not, strictly speaking, start a school. In the suspense that followed his exclusion, Lacan opened and closed this seminar with Spinoza, as he had done with his thesis. In 1932, he referred the "discord" specific to psychosis to a proposition of the *Ethics*; in 1964, he questioned the specific desire of the analyst in relation to Spinoza's exceptional position with respect to human desire. In his act of founding a school, however, Lacan was closer to the classical gesture of the heretic, who, in choosing to take truth from one particular angle, intends to stage a return to the letter of the text against the deviation operated by the institution. Lacan chose to pursue his task of training, a "work in progress" inseparable from his return to Freudian orthodoxy, a task that made him the heretic of the institution, in the manner of modern heresies, which are ecclesial rather than theological.

In his project of improving the statutes in 1953, as much as in his texts of the 1950s, Lacan's reference to an "Ideal Institute" following Freud concerns the teaching programme. On 21 June 1964, in the wake of the seminar on the fundamental concepts of analysis, that is, in the wake of a moment that took on the value of "suspended motion" in the sense of "logical time", Lacan founded the Freudian School of Paris, four weeks after the secret constitution of the French Psychoanalytical Association. He founded it on his own; exclusion had made him truly alone, even with respect to the work of reflection ongoing in the psychoanalytic study group. The text, published under the title *Acte de fondation*, institutionally inscribed the consequences of a return to Freud for training. It undid two splits, which were, in fact, but one. The separation between the two associations, the Paris Psychoanalytical Society (devoted to scientific exchanges), and the Institute (charged with training), was, in effect, an institutional translation of the split between therapeutic and training analyses, one which also organized the hierarchies, both between members of the Society and between them and the trainee analysts at the Institute. Freud had wanted to overcome the differences between healing, researching, and learning. He had stressed that the analytic process was the only place of their "precious encounter". He had also stressed, against received opinion, that the real dividing line was between scientific analysis and its applications, medical or not. He had failed.

Lacan founded a single institution, the working objectives of which were indissociable from the training it dispensed (Lacan, 1965). It was open to non-analysts and included just a single category of membership. Its three sections, and not just the first, which seems to involve "didactics", all share the twin objectives of work and training. The division between the first two sections is as subtle as the one Freud effected in 1926 by trying to undo the split instituted in Berlin and then standardized.

The first section was called "pure analysis, meaning praxis and doctrine of analysis as such". Thus, it included the practice and doctrine of psychoanalysis full stop, as there is only one. Freud insisted that the most "noble" trait and the most joyful aspect (*erfreulichte*) of analytic work is the "scientific gain" (*Wissenschaftlicher Gewinn*): what one can discover and learn in it; the knowledge constructed in it, as much for the analyst as the analysand. This makes analysis as such already didactic. Among "all the issues of didactic analysis", this is the one which makes it the training of the analyst. The "urgent problems" concerning all these issues necessitate the work of those who have experience of "the" didactic; it is a question of shedding light, as much by doctrine as by acquired experience, on what constitutes the praxis of "pure psychoanalysis" as in itself a training. In this praxis, Lacan included the treatment, the effects of teaching, and supervision.

If, through a happy encounter, analytic *praxis* both teaches and treats at the same time, if an analysis is also a treatment, it follows that one can work and train (oneself) in that dimension. The categories and the structures underlying the Freudian praxis would be tested in the clinical work, in the nosographical definitions and in the therapeutic projects in order to effect a critique of the suitability of analysis applied to therapeutics. The doctrine of the treatment and its variations and casuistics will form, together with psychiatric information and medical research, the object of the second section.

The "shift" that this division creates in relation to the split instituted by the IPA is not stable. It takes up the way Freud, in Budapest, distinguished between the "pure gold" of analysis and the alloys needed in its therapeutic application; however, while he separated the two dimensions, Lacan never distinguished two types of analysis. As "pure gold", as "pure technique", according to his expression of 1949, "pure analysis not being in itself a therapeutic technique", no medical qualification can be required to do an analysis which aims at training as a psychoanalyst. For the first time, an institution proposed radically to support lay analysis.

The third section, consisting of "a mapping of the Freudian field", ought to allow, by linking analysis to related sciences, a study of the principles from which it could receive its status in science; a status that would imply not making it an ineffable experience. But, if those sciences inform the analytic experience and its communication, analysis, via its own manner of treating theory, that is, by means of a "praxis of theory" that recognizes the articulation of a subject with knowledge, should also be able to address those sciences in turn and their possible "political drifting". This section includes a continuous commentary on the analytic movement.

With these three sections, the founding text proposed a distribution of work and training such that they were "indissolubly" linked. The choice of this term, where one would have expected "indissociable", and which could make one think of a lapsus, underscores the quality of the link between this aim and the task: like the weft and woof of a fabric, they are impossible to unwind without damaging the cloth of the school. This distribution is as valid for those who "train" as it is for those who "train themselves", who have the same status as "member", and it does not make rules: neither re selection, nor *cursus*, nor technique (a term only appearing once in the text), nor the authorization to practise analysis. No "liberal" had until that point even imagined such deregulation, except Freud. The organization proposed by Lacan "counts simple habits for nought". That is how he settled, some weeks after the foundation, the concerns and questions of those who chose to follow his teaching but were still ruled by those habits. He responded to them with his *Note Adjointe* and the *Préambule* (1965).

The former clarified some of the consequences of this deregulation, the attempt to set up a training regarding which Lacan wrote to Serge Leclaire: " For ten years I have done everything to build a new training, one which would not be a lie" (Roudinesco, 1990, p. 337). To the lie, and the regulation that sustains it, he opposed the facts (thus the "fact" of didactic analysis which always authorizes the trainer *après-coup*), responsibilities (those of the School and those of the new practitioner requiring supervision), and a commitment to work in the School and in psychoanalysis. He also indicated the open questions: the qualification of an analysis as a training analysis, for example. We will return to these points later on. The *Préambule* specified the place of Lacan's teaching: by giving some guarantee to the decision involved in his act, it could be pursued outside of the School. The text further emphasized the responsibility taken by analysis in participating in "the spread of a psychotherapy linked to the needs of social hygiene", that is, its responsibility towards the discontents in civilization.

So Lacan founded a School. Though Freud's term *Hochschule* may have played a part, wittingly or not, Lacan linked his choice to the ancient world. Before the term came to designate the place where a knowledge was taught, a doctrine, and the gathering of people around a master or a style, the Latin *schola* and the Greek *scholê* carried the meaning of a time of respite, of leisure, of a space within the pressing duties of the city, before it signified the studies that might be worthy to fill this space: the liberal arts. In their opposition to *negotium*, they could provide refuge against the discontent of civilization. But the fact that Lacan himself sought refuge for his teaching in a "practical" school, organized into "sections", conceived at its foundation as a "great laboratory", evoking the critical and scientific spirit of the sixteenth and seventeenth centuries against the rhetorical teaching of the university, was not without influence in the choice of the term "school" (Le Brun, 1998). We have hypothesized elsewhere that Lacan's response to his rejection from the field of training by the IPA also bore the trace, perhaps the memory, of George Bataille's initiative in the autumn of 1942 (Tardits, 1998). He had proposed to some friends that they should organize a school on the model of the Hautes Études. With the horizon of "unlimited unhappiness" looming, it was to allow an "inner experience" to be put into concepts and communicated, an experience capable of resisting the fascination of sacrifice.

These references give the scope of the ambition, the promises, and the pitfalls of the founding of Lacan's school. We can see them in the insistence and equivocation of the two terms "work" and "critique". An objective of the school, an object of contract and commitment, work is taken in its scientific sense, thereby including its communication and publication. But this notion, in the Freudian field, cannot be dissociated from the use by Freud of *Arbeit* in relation to the dreamwork and to the work of mourning. Neither can one ignore the modern forms of its exploitation and the worst ideological uses of the term. The notion of "critique" is to be understood in its reference to an autonomous discipline, established during the Renaissance and constitutive, indeed, prerequisite today for any scientific textual practice. It is a recurring reference in Lacan. In order to define "the ungraspable but radical revolution" of Freudianism, he linked it, through the person of Erasmus, to the modification of the "moorings of being" "by changing the procedures of exegesis" (Lacan, 1966, p. 438). In both these revolutions, the relation of man to the signifier had been changed. By means of the *kherem* pronounced against Spinoza, the communitarian and rabbinical authorities of Amsterdam rejected his critical method of reading the Bible. To affirm the validity of the exercise of reason together with a scientific approach to a text put in question the Revelation and its authorized interpreters. But, in Lacan's founding text, the notion of critique is associated with that of "supervision" (*contrôle*), which carries the same ambiguity as "work" in terms of its scientific, social, and analytic senses. Finally, the judgement and choice, indeed the cutting edge of separation implied by critical activity (*krinein*) may evoke the idea of condemnation at play in the denunciation of doctrinal deviations.

These equivocations are at the root of certain "stumbling blocks" which are intimately linked to the "promises" of the founding of the School. If the transference that makes analysis is also a source of resistance and closure of the unconscious, this is because the subject calls on the analyst to incarnate as much the signifier of the ideal in which he locates himself, as a master of truth and knowledge. This wish is fulfilled when the analytic institution organizes itself along the lines of conventional groups (church and army), which Freud analysed via the structure of hypnosis. An object or abstraction can be put in that place of the ideal; a *leader* can also lend himself willingly to this incarnation. Lacan linked the malaise of the analytic community to this group structure in 1956, and sometimes implied that it had been some sort of intention of Freud. But the founding of the School had every chance of putting him in that very position. Two rather martial metaphors in the text suggest an unexpected conjunction of transference and mastery: to consider that the school is a "centre of operations", no longer against the discontents in civilization, but in a "movement of reconquest", a leader might well want to fulfil this mission both as analyst and as chief of an army of "decided workers"! We have seen that Freud, in 1926, tried to counter the effects of the institution he had wanted. Lacan tried to preserve the School from these pitfalls, as much by means of the particular desire which leads an analyst to undo this conjunction, to which he is called by the analysand, of transference with mastery, as by the activation of two mechanisms of the school introduced to counter these pitfalls. The paradoxical relations of the subject to desire and knowledge do not fail to have effects within the institution and, in return, the institution can be a barrier to their treatment in analysis. By recognizing the connections of thought to desire and the singular outcome of the transference that is the desire of the analyst, the mechanisms of the cartel and the *pass* were going to try to allow a new and different training of the analyst. (For the history of the EFP, see Roudinesco, 1990, pp. 381–477, 633–677.)

CHAPTER FIVE

The Training of the School

In order to explore the logic of the new training Lacan expected from his school, "a new training that would not be a lie", we have chosen to follow the divisions of the three sections of the Freudian School of Paris to the letter. These divisions did not distinguish between work, research, and training; they did not retain the differentiation between basic and further training current in professional trainings. In 1965, the cartels were recorded in the School's annual according to these sections; the preparatory work for the first Study Days of 1966 was grouped along the same lines.

Related knowledge

In 1953, the malaise in relation to training was not confined to France or localized only in the discords of power; it touched on the very transmission of knowledge. Robert Knight related it to the absence of a master, the number of candidates, and their mediocrity: they do not read, they only want to finish their training as quickly as possible, and they are more interested in the clinic than in research and theory (Knight, 1953, quoted by Lacan, 1966, p. 295

[the references to the *Écrits* are designated *E*]). Lacan did not reject these remarks, but, for him, they did not identify the real root of the evil: "pre-digested" knowledge taught in the institution has no value as training; when knowledge aims at systematizing rather than real formalization, its transmission has effects of "disintellectualization". Knowledge, then, remains subject to effects of imaginary capture, more concerned with the "deposition" of experience than in its "mainsprings"; everyone can "poach there to their hearts' content", and technique becomes dull and worn down. This capture is particularly evident in research, in which analysts have lost themselves in a beyond of discourse, making of the imaginary the norm of the real, where Freud had tried to distinguish them by subordinating the imaginary to symbolic determination. To misrecognize this determination produces a form of analphabetism: the major forms of the unconscious (the word-with-word of metonymy, the word-for-word of metaphor) and the syntax of the phrase of the phantasy, which alone can "free the augury from its desire for entrails", are cast aside in favour of psychological fantasies, which vary with fashion.

The institutional choices of the 1920s were responsible, according to Lacan, for this abandoning of a rational foundation for the specificity of analysis, as much in the system of sciences as in the practices of care. The "biologistic" or "culturalist" tendencies of theory misrecognize the fact that analytic concepts are not based in biology or sociology, even if these are neighbouring disciplines. If one forgets that the analytic experience, the most vital terms of which are the unconscious and sexuality, is based on speech and is situated, as Freud emphasized, at "the abyss separating the bodily from the psychical", one cannot formulate the alterity of analysis that its recognition requires, nor allow theory to free itself from its capture by a clinic of the gaze.

At the same time, Lacan linked the basic concepts of technique, "already powerfully articulated between themselves" by Freud, and which constituted, within training, the "spirit of a tradition", to the effects of language. If the treatment is a practice of reading and writing of the unconscious text carried by the speech of the analysand, then the training of the analyst cannot misrecognize what the truth of the unconscious owes to "the letter of language", nor that, "the register of truth is to be taken literally" (*E*, pp. 305, 391). Of course, the analyst already learns this in his own analysis, but it is essential that he be instructed in the knowledge and know-how of other practices of the letter. Just as one does not do algebra without knowing how to write, operating with the symbolic implies knowing what are facts of speech and facts of writing.

The principle of "liberally conceived studies", put forward by Lacan in 1953, might seem ambiguous. One could see it as a liberal position in relation to the autocratic regulation of a *cursus* through which an analyst "is trained" (Lacan, 1976, p. 54). Yet, the stress was on the "discipline" that these studies, brought into the service of a science qualified as "humanistic", would allow one to gain rather than on the free enterprise of "training oneself". The liberal would therefore refer to the "liberal arts" of the medieval university: the Trivium (grammar, rhetoric, logic) and the Quadrivium (geometry, arithmetic, astronomy, music). In his *Rome Discourse*, Lacan declared himself ready to endorse these "somewhat old-fashioned" headings, to which Freud had referred in his hope that analysis might link medicine with the *universitas literarum* and philosophy (*E*, p. 238). The moment Lacan dealt with the poorly handled problem of the formalization which might allow analysis to take up its place among the sciences, he began a return to these sources, a return to what was "the re-creation of human meaning in an arid era of scientism" (*E*, pp. 235–239). To these practices of the letter, to which Freud had added mythology and literature, Lacan would add the figures of the sophist, the story-teller, the Talmudist, the poet, the exegete, and the philologist. To which one could add also the critic and the translator.

It is because of the recognized affinity of these practices that Lacan could "authorise himself to practice a literal commentary on Freud", allowing himself to be "guided by Freud's letter" without either worship or superstition (*E*, p. 304). This was the aim of the "textual seminars" devoted to reading Freud's texts, which were an issue in the institutional confrontation of 1953, and the spirit of which Lacan kept alive in a time when translations of his work were either absent or faulty. In recognition of these "affinities", Lacan could invite linguists, philosophers and mathematicians to his seminar, as well as the texts of writers. Similarly, he could extract teaching material from certain texts in order to introduce the study of major topics: Plato and Paul Claudel for the transference,

Shakespeare for the place of desire, Sophocles for ethics, Blanchot for the object little *a*, Duras for the knot of phantasy, Joyce for the knot of the *sinthome*. The idea was not to "broaden minds" or to cultivate the analysts, initiating them in the "humanities". Yet, these themes would not be negligible: the "not-knowing" which has a central place in theory, as in experience, is not a "void of thought" and "learned ignorance" is not "saintly ignorance". But they are secondary in relation to the real stake of these affinities between analysis and related domains of knowledge.

Through listening to the symptom and the unconscious, Freud discovered the structural reason why the literality of a text, sacred or profane, increases in importance the more it involves an encounter with truth (*E*, p. 304). In the treatment a subject can come to recognize, in the symbolic chain which makes up the law of his destiny and his desire, the "fragment of discourse" of which he has made himself "the living alphabet", he can come closer to seeing how the real of sexuality takes part in the effect of truth given in the unconscious and the symptom. How can one think that part? There, where Freud spoke of an abyss, Lacan noted that the cause of the subject's desire is only linked to sex in an "oblique way"; he would later formulate that the sexual relation cannot be written. If Freud, talking about "what can" be transmitted of psychoanalysis, posited the principle of a limit of transmission, this limit has less to do with people or the state of knowledge than with the aversion of thought (including that of analysts) to the object of analysis. This aversion has to do with the fact, also noted by Foucault, that letting the sexual enter into thought is to take thought to its limits. Analysis both recognizes and tries to push beyond this limit and aversion; it is with this attempt to think the incidence of the signifier on the sexed living being that Lacan encountered other fields of knowledge, let himself be taught by them, utilized and questioned them.

The critique levelled by Lacan at humanism can explain the paradoxical and close relation he had with these domains of knowledge: he emphasized, through the figure of Erasmus, the importance of humanism in action (*E*, p. 438). In moving from the theological commentary of a text to the critical study of the letter, by applying a rational reading to the signifiers of the sacred text, Erasmus subverted the procedures of exegesis. In his prudent desire to lay down a stable basis for the establishment of the text, this scholar, hardly formed for political battles, revolutionized the relation of man to the discourse that shaped him. The relation to the authority of the master was changed. Not only was the validity of the use of reason with a text justified and demonstrated, but, in the institutions, this textual practice took on a priority over the teachings of the authorized clerics. A "horizontal" society of humanists was created, a "republic of letters", different from the hierarchies of power and knowledge, together with the technical tools for diffusing these practices: to read the text one needs the book, the rigorous and precise publication of the text. For each person is concerned with the letter of the text and not only its commentary, however judicious. By thus modifying everything that anchored man, humanism contributed to the formation of the modern science of the letter, but it also incurred a debt: a debt, belief, and promise to found within man himself an ethic and governance of men.

Within man means within speech, a speech that could also belong to madness: "It is Folly speaking", and Folly says "I" (Erasmus, 1993, p. 9). At this moment, when the domain of the sciences was not yet established, when the great divide between reason and unreason was not yet mapped out, the ambiguous praise of folly recognized its determination in the field of laughter, play, transmission of life, the search for the secrets of the universe, action, and society itself. But the debt thus established was "irredeemably contested" by subsequent humanist discourse, which did not know how to link to speech and to its laws the destiny of man, that question the subject encounters when placed in a new way in front of the enigma of his sex and his existence.

By listening to what returns from the field of enjoyment excluded by science, and by touching on the relation of man to the signifier, analysis, in its turn, has created a debt. Will analysts know not to contest it? Lacan's long immersion in related domains of knowledge is also explained by the necessity of articulating speech and language to questions of desire and being, the enigma of sex, to the real of men *and* women. Hence his interest in philosophers who questioned being, a question which the neurotic *is* "in himself, completely, from head to toe, the question and the asking of it" (Lacan, 1957). (In his book, *Ce que Lacan dit de l'être*, Balmès [1999] reviews ten years of the journey Lacan spent shaping some key notions.) That is the reason that Freudian materialism, unlike natural materialism, cannot strip the subject of his history. Operating on this subject, whose specific mode of constitution is determined by modern science, requires an articulation of truth, understood as a signifying material cause, to the real of enjoyment and the letter. That is what Lacan tried to impart in the twenty-five years of his teaching, the "praxis of theory" functioning as an ethics that was alert to the dimension of jouissance. To restore the symbolic chain that overdetermines a subject in the dimensions "of history of a life lived as history" is one of the ways Lacan, in 1957, understood the training of the analyst (E, p. 366).

During the 1950s, when he had finished exploring the imaginary dimension of the ego with which he developed the "social" factor of his first ternary construction of 1932 (individual, social, structural), Lacan endeavoured to theorize the cut that determines for the subject the heteronymy of the symbolic. Hence he developed the "structural dimension" he had aimed at in his thesis. In order to pursue the programme of formalization of the dimensions of experience set out in the *Rome Discourse*, he primarily appealed to structural linguistics, like Lévi-Strauss, but also to mathematics and logic. If the figures and tropes of language are required to grasp the different modalities of defence, that is, the rejection of truth, the Saussurian distinction between signifier and signified was the basis needed to train analysts in the problematics of language. With this "initiatory reference", Lacan could free the unconscious from a theory that substantialized it, breaking with the organicism, dynamic or not, which haunted psychology, and thus return to the psychic apparatus the way Freud had conceived it, as a series of inscriptions and translations existing only because of language. By ordering the phonetic and syntactic systems of language, linguistics allows one to uncover the structure of all thought; knowledge of language allowed Lacan to ground the specific aspect of the Freudian unconscious, its "formations" (including the symptom), and the "culture" that analytic discourse makes of this unconscious. By formulating the intimate link between the symbolic and death, Lacan loosened the hold of biology on the death drive.

This endeavour to formalize was underpinned by a "doctrinal of science", that is, the "conjunction of propositions on science and propositions on the subject", thus including analysis in a Galileism extended to contemporary structuralisms (Milner, 1995, pp. 33–37 attempts to bring out its axioms). Already, in 1953, Lacan stressed how modern science produced a new mode of constituting a subject, which he localized ten years later in the *cogito* of Descartes. His conjecture of a modern science of the letter, effecting a break with the "épistème" of antiquity, specified the subject as pure subject of a signifier, divided from "himself", that is, between the signifier representing him and which he is equivalent to, and his being, which falls away and which Lacan pinpointed with object little *a*. He also described the particular alienation which results from rejecting truth and the exclusion of the field of enjoyment which this produces. With the algebra of the subject and the *cogito* of Descartes, he developed the supposition of the subject and of knowledge in the transference, the logic of the phantasy that analysis has to construct, the logic of the analytic act, all in all, the essential mainsprings of an experience which takes signifying determination and the field of enjoyment into account. Using mathematical logic and the "matheme", he wrote the "discourses", the name he gave to the forms of social bond which are characterized by a certain structure (discourse of the master, of the hysteric, of the university and of the analyst, as well as the version of the discourse of the master that constitutes the discourse of capitalism). He also wrote the formulas of sexuation, that is, the choice the speaking being has of counting himself as man or woman in relation to the phallic function and to castration. (On these writings, see Revue Littoral, 1992; Milner, 1995; Nawawi, 1999.)

It is paradoxical that Lacan's long exploration of the letter led him to aim at an integral and unequivocal transmission of knowledge developed for a practice which worked with equivocation. Lacan's formalizations necessitated a theory of the letter which had for long been but poorly distinguished from the signifier. The work with formalization renewed the question, recognized early on, of its relation to the sexual (the letter feminizes), with the body (that of the letter, and the body that writes); Lacan in the end came to see the letter as analogous to the germen which carries life and death together in bodies (Lacan, 2000, p. 97). To some extent, the edge through which a letter partakes of the real also led him to another writing, the writing of the Borromean knot, which, in its autonomy in relation to the signifier, would attempt to circumscribe the real of human beings.

It is important to note the recurring references to biological knowledge in these "Borromean" years. This knowledge, recommended by Freud in the training of analysts, was in some ways neglected by Lacan during the years in which he stressed the primacy of the signifier and the gap between nature and culture, thus privileging the signifying combinatory of sexual exchanges based on symbolic alliances as opposed to natural generation. Yet, the question of what the symbolic owes to death (*E*, p. 316) remained open, as did the question of what the arrival of the signifier in the world of humanity owes to the integration of elementary structures of social functioning to sexual reality (Lacan, 1991, p. 138). The Borromean writing maintains the radical distinction between desire, which can be articulated in signifiers, the imaginary of the body and the real of sex, of the life and death that make up an individual body and which the biologist questions. It aims, however, to write how they hold together, how something real knots body and language, but also how it is a "speaking individual" which supports the hypothesis of the unconscious and hence of the subject (Lacan, 2000, pp. 141–143). Distinct from the ego, to which the subject of psychological development is equated, distinct from the subject of speech, the individual of the first ternary of 1932 here takes its place in this development as the "biological individual", as real; in so far as he is "affected by the unconscious" he is the subject of the signifier (*E*, p. 743; Lacan, 2000, p. 142). In a certain way and at the end of a long redevelopment, the Borromean writing tried to rewrite, in terms of the triad Real–Symbolic–Imaginary, the first triad, individual–subject–social; and now Lacan could republish his 1932 thesis.

Among the related but distinct branches of knowledge that Freud recommended in 1926 for the training of analysts, were biology and the science of sexual life. These were the two registers of knowledge on sex formed in the nineteenth century. In his *Postscript* of 1927, only biology remained. It would be interesting to relate this gap in Freud's two references, that is, the disappearance of the science of sexual life, to the shrewd reading Foucault makes of the *scientia sexualis* (Foucault, 1998). Taking analysis, without naming it, as a prototype of the discourse which he termed *scientia sexualis*, retroactively allowed him to recognize psychoanalysis while denying it its specificity. During the Borromean years, there was a recurring reference to the knowledge that biology tries to situate in the real of sex. At the same time, Lacan formulated in different ways that there is no sexual rapport that can be written. To articulate this impossibility, which makes up the real of human beings, involved contesting the phantasy behind the "will to know" of the *scientia sexualis* . . . but surely not the desire of Freud.

One cannot evoke Lacan's way of bringing related domains of knowledge into proximity with analysis without indicating the paradoxes of this proximity. Freud, to his surprise, had to admit that his investigation of dreams had a link to the lay conception of them, which, even if "half involved in superstition", was closer to the truth than the medical view (Freud, 1901a, p. 635). He did not shrink from identifying the formations of the unconscious as the products of the activity of thought, thereby developing new ideas about thinking itself. Lacan took the step of identifying this thought work with a knowledge, "the knowledge there is in speaking one's language", and which if neglected is in danger of opening the way to all forms of obscurantism. The recourse to knowledge constructed according to the laws of language, and with them, is necessary to the analyst to counter this slippery slope, as is also the reference to the philosophical tradition, indeed the theological one, of a discourse on being and the subject (Balmès, 1999 studies Lacan's close relation to this discourse). Lacan could say that he used these bits of knowledge "as they came to him". The liberty he took in his use of them shows that sometimes what he said was not analogical. To construct an object of knowledge, the unknown knowledge recognized by Freud, took him in the direction of exploring the gaps in other fields of knowledge and to privilege mathematics, which he considered the "most subjective of the sciences". In some of these encounters of Lacan, something of the order of a grafting of knowledge occurs. This happened above all at the point where Lacan located the paradoxes in these fields of knowledge, or when he himself made use of them paradoxically. In these moments of aporia one can "grasp the limits, the impasses, and dead ends that show the real acceding to the symbolic" (Lacan, 2000, p. 93). The work of writing gives co-ordinates to these points; like "the textual work issuing from the belly of the spider", it is "what holds bodies together invisibly".

Analysis applied to therapeutics.

Lacan established the institution of lay analysis. But he also battled against both the marginalization of analysis by medicine and against the social and scientific position of extra-territoriality in which analysts put themselves. He argued that analysis was not "in itself" a therapeutic technique, draw the consequence that no medical qualification was required to become an analyst, and yet advised certain analysands to study medicine. The title of the second section indicates a position different from Freud's concerning applied analysis. Lacan did take up Freud's division between analysis as such, "pure", scientific and research-oriented, involving teaching, and applied analysis. Freud applied it to treatments, works of art, the facts of civilization; for Lacan, it was "applied" only to the treatment: applied analysis "means therapeutic and pertaining to the medical clinic".

The subsections "Doctrine of the treatment and its variants" and "Casuistics" were designed to counter the prevalent psychological bent in relation to the clinic. As well as taking account of the position of the subject in structure, the analytic clinic also focuses on the singular text of each analysand, with what, in so-called free association, is said with the utmost necessity, thus allowing for the isolation of "what is most particular for the subject". The analytical developments on the strategies of the subject in neurosis, perversion, and psychosis, and also the dimensions Lacan uncovered of the Real, Symbolic, and Imaginary are necessary to this orientation. The teaching that Lacan truly "devoted" to the training of analysts susceptible of applying the "desire of the analyst" to the treatment had a different emphasis from the Freudian development. A large part of the seminars was consecrated to redeveloping Freudian metapsychology with the structural approach offered by the laws of language and to try to integrate into it the Freudian versions of the Father (those of the myth of Oedipus and *Totem and Taboo*, and of *Moses and Monotheism*). But an equally important part had as its goal the doctrine of the treatment, the development of its "mainsprings" and its aims, its operation, and "that with which" an analysis operates on a subject. To make a true resolution of the transference possible means thinking about its handling. At a time when the proper domain of analysis was defined as the "field of truth", the handling of the transference was developed by means of the place of the Other, which allowed the neutralizing of the lures of hysterical and obsessional stratagems for "skirting the question" of sex and being. When Lacan unmasked the collusion with truth, the transference was theorized with the supposition of knowledge included in the hypothesis of a subject of the unconscious; confronted with the dimensions of desire and enjoyment, its handling has to take account of the singularity of the relation to the object in the phantasy and the temporal dimension of the subject.

Lacan showed how analysis, as a "practice subordinated by its purpose to what is most particular about the subject", can necessitate, as Freud's discussion of the Wolf man case showed, the putting into question of analytic science in each case (*E*, pp. 296–297). By putting this requirement of particularity under the rubric of casuistics, he emphasized the active dimension of the treatment rather than the horizon of a clinical psychology. The huge body of casuistic literature developed in the sixteenth and seventeenth centuries aimed at the study of situations, particular circumstances determining the application (or not) of a moral, religious, or civil law. The object of the study could be a decision to be made, advice to be given, but also setting of a precedent, for example: when encountering a problem, an individual or a confessor could consult a casuist, who himself could consult another with more experience. As a "Science" of action, casuistics has contributed to the development of calculating probabilities on the one hand, while the biographical stories it generated helped to form the literary genre of the novel. The great case histories of Freud are contemporary with the apogee of the novel; the absence of case histories in Lacan goes hand in hand with the crisis of the novel (Gagey & Gagey, 1990; Le Brun, 2004). Though Lacan borrowed from the Freudian case histories, as part of the psychiatric training that led him to write the case of Aimée, he took from casuistics the necessity of a science of the "mainspring" of action and *kairos*. If, when teaching, he exceptionally brought up the particulars of a case, it was to illustrate what in the treatment constituted the occasion, the right moment, to let the patient know something (*E*, pp. 630–632). His development of the analytic act and the unusual "social bond" that analytic treatment offers the patient was inscribed in this casuistry.

The suitability, or not, of analysis was affected by this. One clinical tradition calculates the possibility of analysis by taking into account the conditions of transference, time, payment, age, and culture, but also the risk that a patient might be submerged by drives and fantasies, and the probability of healing the symptom. The selection of candidates derived from a similar assessment. Placing analysis within the field of truth, the quest for meaning or the construction of knowledge, the opening of a gap between demand and desire, the development of the subject's temporality and the emphasis given to the act in focusing the transference, were all factors which determined a different approach to probability. For the precedent of suitability was substituted the offer of an encounter, contingent by definition, with analysis. The practice of preliminary sessions was also modified by this, as a longer period of these was necessary to refine the diagnosis and transforms the prognosis of suitability for analysis.

The problematic of suitability and differential diagnosis required by medical precedent was a determining factor in Freud's failure in 1927. Without a sufficiently clear theory of the psychic mechanism of psychosis, he had to bow to the prudence of his students who asked for a medical diagnosis prior to analytic treatment. The articulation of the concept of foreclosure of the Name-of-the-Father allowed the obstacle Freud encountered in his plea for lay analysis to be surmounted. Linking the defence mechanisms proper to psychosis to the laws of language, the signifying organization and the grammatical tropes of negation gave the possibility for analysis "as such" to resist less to psychotic speech (Lacan, 2006j).

Despite these clinical advances, Lacan did not think he was quits with medicine; he hoped for a critical dialogue in which medics and psychiatrists could question analysts regarding symptoms and nosographical definitions. But the manner in which he addressed himself as "missionary of the doctors" to the doctors in the Hospital of Sick Children, who made a place for analysis in their team, manifests a clear reversal of reference. The round table discussion organized in 1966 by Aubry gave Lacan the occasion to formulate how Freud's discovery could allow the doctor to respond to the subversion of his traditional position through the progress of science (Aubry et al., 1966). Dislodged from his ancient sacred function by the conjunction between this progress and the social requirement to administer public health in an economic manner, a doctor can remain so only if he recognizes that he acts within the register of the patient's demand (to get well) and his desire (to preserve the symptom which holds him together, for example). Confronted with the demands of a new production of health, the sale of organs, the addictive use of drugs, he would not be able to respond if he did not take account of the "real body", the one of enjoyment, exiled by the Cartesian dichotomy between thought and extension, one which requires an ethical dimension. The dialogue was difficult.

During the years of the Freudian School of Paris, and even the French Society of Psychoanalysis, the relation between the training of analysts and psychiatric knowledge, was more dialectical (Roudinesco, 1990, pp. 192, 478–488). The 1950s had been marked by three facts. Synthetic pharmacology heralded a renewal of therapeutics that, thirty years later, was going to undo psychiatric knowledge, already shaken by its contradictory alliances with neurology and analysis. Divergent in their orientations and their reforms, institutional psychotherapy and the politics of psychiatric sectorization had tried to humanize psychiatric incarceration and to integrate analysis. Lacan confirmed his break with organodynamism by linking the psychotic mechanism of defence with the processes of language. At Bonneval in 1960, Ey invited philosophers, psychiatrists, and psychoanalysts from the French Society, as well as the Psychoanalytic Society of Paris, to a conference on the status of the unconscious; he recognized its importance for psychiatrists in training, who also formed the main public for the theoretical jousts on the relation between the unconscious and language. In 1961, Foucault in his *History of Madness* (2006) made himself "apostle and exegete" of a form of unreason separated from its language; this was a move against the will to silence madness and to objectify it into mental illness. If Ey thought the book "psychiatricidal", Lacan recognized that this great work, by means of its critical–historical method, situated the "responsibility of medicine in the great ethical crisis (that is, touching on the definition of man)" equated by Foucault with the "isolation of madness" (Aubry et al., 1966, p. 765). These different factors orientated psychiatrists in training towards analysis, and a great number became analysts. At the same time, young lay analysts undertook the encounter with madness in the institutions that allowed its speech: the clinic of La Borde, opened in 1953 by Jean Oury, and the Experimental School of Bonneuil, founded by Maud Mannoni in 1970. The 1967 October conference on infantile psychoses was an important moment in these encounters between psychiatry and analysis; Lacan paid homage to the civilizing work of Ey (Mannoni, 1976, 1984). In November of that same year, he addressed the trainee psychiatrists of St Anne hospital in the context of the Circle of Psychiatric Studies set up with Ey in 1966 (transcribed with the title "Petit discours aux psychiatres", unpublished).

In October 1968, the EFP chose the theme of the relations between analysis and psychotherapy for its conference. It meant bringing up the dialectical tension between the therapeutic and the analytic within each treatment, a tension emphasized by Freud when he recognized the necessary detour through the transference neurosis and the suspension of the therapeutic aim. It meant circumscribing the new context of this relation, which had become paradoxical when the normative injunction of health and prevention turned the traditional psychotherapeutic dimension of medicine into a mass phenomenon. These social, economic, and ideological co-ordinates accentuated the heterogeneity between analysis and the psychotherapies. Analysis holds that one ought to complete the symptom rather than remove it in order to render it analysable, to recognize that the complaint of someone who suffers and demands to be healed can cover a desire not to get better which is sustained by a phantasmatic relation to the object that would have the power to heal. The treatment of the symptom and the complaint is heterogeneous with practices that, in misrecognizing the anchorage of the symptom in the symbolic dimension and enjoyment, the gap between desire and demand, can, when seeking the best, lead to the worst. Yet, despite the heterogeneity, these two orders of practice do meet, in a problematic manner, in healthcare institutions, particularly those concerned with the care of children. In the paper concluding the conference, Lacan asked if the practice of psychotherapy supposedly inspired by analysis should be considered as a step in the training of the analyst, and what its occurrence might be in so-called training analysis, in the limits such analysis encounters and which could make it run aground. We will see that this question is crucial in thinking about supervision.

Hospital consultations and clinical presentations became an important element in training because of the confrontation it provided between analysis, medicine, and psychiatry. Those of Françoise Dolto at Trousseau and those of Jenny Aubry at the Sick Children's Hospital were particularly apt for developing the specific conditions of child analysis: the intervention of a real third party, taking the parents into account in the handling of the transference, given the place the child reserves for them, the situating of symptoms in relation to infantile neurosis, and the neurotic structure established subsequently. During the conference on transmission in 1978, a round table discussion was devoted to the "effects of transmission of analysis through the attendance of analysts in training" at Dolto's consultations. This latter had asked the question of the opportune moment in the training to attend these consultations; analysts gave evidence of the effect it might have on their analysis and their relation to theory. Several pointed out how Dolto's capacity to admit to not understanding, in front of the children and the public, had effects of transmission.

This was a detail also emphasized by the analysts present at Lacan's clinical presentations. He had kept this practice going, inherited from a long tradition in medical and psychiatric training. Charcot's lessons at La Salpetrière are a reference here; Freud was present at them, admiring the talents of Charcot, now doctor, now professor, now researcher, and always magisterial; seduced by the gestural and vocal theatricality, he was interested in the nosographical research into the laws and classifications which gave hysteria a scientific status and no longer limited it to women (Braud, 1998). Very likely he was thinking of this when he noted in 1916 that, contrary to medical teaching which gave to see, and to psychiatric teaching, which could allow the complaint about a symptom to be heard, "analytic treatment did not allow an audience"; transference ruled this out. Therefore, one could only know analysis through one's own experience or hearsay (Freud, 1915–1917, p. 15). Students of Lacan, however, sometimes analysands who attended his clinical presentations, insisted on their effects of transmission (Czermak, 1987; Miller, 1977b; Porge, 1985). Lacan's know-how in engaging a very tight dialogue which would allow a real encounter (having consequences for the subject), his way of allowing himself to be taken, surprised, signalling his incomprehension, and of submitting entirely to "the properly subjective positions" of the patient without reducing them to a morbid process (*E*, p. 447), doubtless created the conditions for showing a real which could not be spoken. That the interlocutor of choice was the psychotic is certainly structural. The way of inserting an invisible barrier, excluding all complicity, between the dialogue and the public offered a space in which the signifiers of the subject's unconscious scenario could emerge and form a demand. A major effect of training seems to have been that each of the three protagonists of the event was a subject, taught and affected by a knowledge derived from psychotic speech. This knowledge carried a question, which Lacan's development of the narcissistic alienation of the ego, the heteronomy of the symbolic, and the real as impossible responded to: "Why does a normal man, so-called, not realise that speech is a parasite?" (Lacan, 1975–1976, pp. 91–102). In other words: why are we not crazy?

Supervision, instituted in Berlin and then regulated within the IPA to guide the new analyst in conducting the treatment and to authorize his practice, should logically have been included in this section of "applied analysis". Against all expectation, Lacan did not place it there, but incorporated it into "pure analysis", thus initiating a radically different approach to the practice of supervision.

Pure analysis

Freud's desire was decisive in giving up hypnosis despite its therapeutic results and in the inaugural act of "analysing", the *Analysieren*, which he would in the end describe as an impossible profession. Yet, a long time was needed before the question of the desire of the analyst was posed in the training. In this time, Lacan's hypothesis concerning the part of death within language allowed him, when linking the analytic training to the second topography, to effect a return to Freud within the field of this question. Almost as a necessity, the idea which isolated "the" didactic analysis by placing it at the beginning of a learning *cursus*, colluded with a wanting-to-be-an-analyst and conceived of the end of such an analysis as an identification with the analyst. Yet, when not challenged, this wanting and this identification foil the analysis, which alone can challenge them. To want to be in the position of having the last word, which could be a figure of a wanting-to-know at the root of the choice of profession, can be as much of an internal obstacle as the intrusion of professional and institutional reality when they form the horizon, indeed the present, of a training analysis. To want to conform, to know, have the knowledge and the power that can result from it, echo the choice of the subject of not wanting to know anything of the truth and prevent a knowledge being constructed by means of unconscious knowledge. And yet it is this knowledge of structure that can work in reserve, so that another person—the analysand—can construct it with his own unconscious knowledge.

Doubtless one had to renounce "the" didactic and the *cursus* accompanying it in order to articulate the "training function" of an analysis: in the widest sense, what it teaches an analysand, the knowledge it allows one to construct, and in a mere specific sense, the training of the analyst that it makes possible. The analyst can take his place as a particular product in this "culture" of the unconscious, of its formations, that an analysis is. Whether understood as a new "flower of Tarbes" or one of those "blue flowers" that grow in the remains of history, or instead as a training [formation] of analysis as a geological formation, the analyst is no more the result of a "one trains [forms]" than of a "training [forming] oneself". One can only know in retrospect that an analysis was didactic in this narrow sense and that the analyst was a "trainer". Lacan could say, in 1973, that he would have liked to give up these terms, but he kept their use for an analysis that would open on to its own act, as opposed to the establishment (Lacan, 1970a, p. 20). The subversion he effected in 1964 allows and requires one to rethink the training of the analyst in relation both to the end of the treatment and to the "school training", to be understood in the sense of "musical training". By arguing that the "long subjective ascesis" that analysis is must be "uninterrupted" to its end, Lacan continued in the tradition of Ferenczi; yet his compass point was the last question in Freud's text "Analysis terminable and interminable" (1937c).

During the crisis with Rank in 1924, Freud had formulated in his letter to the Committee the importance of letting the pupils doing a training analysis live through "as many of their inner processes as possible" (Jones, 1957, p. 64). He was convinced that Rank had been destabilized by his practice as much as the news of his master's cancer. Ferenczi was going to radicalize Freud's advice by generalizing the hope for systematic analyses pushed to their end. Freud rather supported the notion of *Nachtragsanalysen*, as Jones would that of "postgraduate analysis" (Paskaukas, 1993, pp. 729–731). Responding to the impasses in which the institutional framework put training analyses, the practice of "post training", or private and even secret analyses became widespread. In 1953, Balint noted that this practice put the training system in question and prevented an eventual theoretical development of the analysis of the analyst: was this secret practice followed in the manner of Ferenczi's "supertherapy", and with what result? Was the aim "research" (Balint, 1952) instead? Lacan thought that the "impenetrable darkness" surrounding training analyses and its aims and conditions was the source of the silence which reigned in the institution (*E*, p. 399). A true institutional symptom, which he mocked in 1956, this silence seemed ignorant of the terms of the posthumous debate publicly started by Freud with Ferenczi in 1937.

Ferenczi's conference speech at Innsbruck in 1927 was his clinical and theoretical contribution to the debate on lay analysis (Ferenczi, 1982). Starting from a patient's character trait—the tendency to lie—and considering that it extended to the various distortions of facts and to disobeying the fundamental rule, he uncovered the phantasmatic dimension of the trait and held that the neurosis was structured by this "lie" that was the unconscious phantasy. Analysis must, therefore, explore the unconscious phantasmatic structure which was precipitated during repression and which he called "character"; it has to separate the real from the phantasy. A therapeutic analysis is only finished if it is an analysis of character, allowing its "re-crystallization" after dissolution of its first "crystalline" structure. This requires time, repetition, and working-through, and tact in handling the transference. This last condition requires that the "analyst himself has completely finished his own analysis"; it presupposes that one has mourned the unconscious phantasmatic colouring which has crept into the treatment, that a man has vanquished the castration complex and a woman the virility complex. The text showed Ferenczi's refusal to distinguish therapeutic and training analyses and gave the status he accorded a year later to the analysis of the analyst: the "second fundamental rule", it was the "only viable basis for sound analytic technique" (Ferenczi, 1955).

This "substantial " and ambitious text of Ferenczi's, as well as his reproach to Freud for not having analysed thoroughly, form a key reference in "Analysis terminable and interminable" (Freud, 1937c). Freud intended to "stir up" discussion with other analysts, but also with himself. He contested the ambition to rival fate by making latent conflicts actual in the treatment and preferred recognizing the limits analysis accepted by renouncing hypnosis, but he did take up the idea that analysis of the analyst, as distinct from therapeutic analyses, had to be analysis of character. This is due to the danger that working with the unconscious poses to the analyst and the practical necessity of excluding all make-believe, of recognizing truth and reality. He admitted that in the case of a character analysis, the effective end could approach that envisaged by theory. The theory postulates, demands even, that analysis can operate "a retroactive correction of the original process of repression" which would put an end to the excessive strength of a drive. The end of analysis is not, therefore, the end that would complete the form given at the outset, according to the classic scheme of a *Bildung*. But one is forced to confront what one does not want to see: the transformation of the mechanism of defence is often incomplete. Freud suspected that the analyst could not arrive at this end by means of the anticipated alliance with a "normal" ego and preferred to acknowledge the obstacles standing in the way of this collective aim: the pathogenic modification of the ego through the defence mechanisms, the more or less greater proximity with the psychotic ego, remains of some archaic inheritance, effects of the death drive, and last, something not recognized by Ferenczi, the "rock of castration", that is, the refusal, of man or woman, of femininity. Freud did not directly deal with the question of phantasy which was at the heart of Ferenczi's argument, but he situated the fixation of "character" as an effect in the ego of those mechanisms of defence which sacrifice truth by falsifying it, particularly the perception of the dangers of the drive encountered by the ego in distress.

Lacan has made no reference to Ferenczi's text, yet he could not have ignored it. (He quotes the article on the elasticity of technique that he describes as "luminous" and highlights the error in Reich's character analysis [*E*, pp. 282–285].) He never commented on the whole of Freud's text, but regularly referred to its main question, interpreting the irreducible rock of castration sometimes as Freud stopping at the edge of the promised land and sometimes as an impasse. Since he stated his opposition to the didactic end of analysis conceived as identification with the ego of the analyst ("If one trains analysts it is so that there can be subjects whose ego is absent" [Lacan, 1990b, p. 246]), he focused on developing this rock as a fundamental relation of the subject to the phallus and not as a biological rock. To think through the antinomies encountered by the human being in the process of taking on their sex, that is, the vagaries of the castration complex in men and of *Penisneid* in women, was going to require the articulation of the phallus to language and its effects, to the dimensions of being and having. The impasse structured by the dilemma *having–not-having* the phallus would be resolved if the subject could realize, in analysis, that he *is* not the phallus which, as signified, gives the signification of the desire of the mother, and, as signifier of desire, is called on to make up for the lack of the signifier in the Other that would say what the subject is. This presupposes that analysis can touch that being of the subject which the passions of love, hate, and ignorance invariably aim to realize, and, thus, that which he is not, in so far as he is only an effect of language. This involves confronting the disarray produced by the lack of response, the vertigo of questioning the use of the signifier as such, the anxiety arising when the being of the subject as such is approached, and the distress of man in "his relation to himself which is his own death". (The articulation of the question of the phallus to that of the object is slowly elaborated in the seminars dedicated to the ethics of psychoanalysis, transference, identification, and anxiety.) Taking on castration thus introduces another modality of the end of the analysis of the analyst, first formulated by Lacan: the subjectivization of death, a process which does not derive from any knowledge nor from anything imaginable (*E*, p. 289). These two modalities of the end of analysis anticipate the recognition, which is just as problematic, of sexual non-rapport.

At the point where the problematic of the being of the subject, formulated with the object *a*, is linked to castration, Lacan, in some sense inevitably, encountered Ferenczi's intuition concerning the crucial role played by unconscious phantasy. A support of desire, the phantasy keeps the remainder of enjoyment which escapes the signifying process at a distance; covering over the refused truth of castration and screening off the real, it is a decisive element in the "space of defence in which the subject is organised" (*E*, p. 195), and it allows the subject to misrecognize that it is only an effect of the signifier. Thinking about the analytic operation and its results thus made it necessary for Lacan to think through the relation of the subject to the object, and not only to the phallus, and the way the analyst places himself in relation to them. He did this in his teaching by means of the algebra of the subject. It allowed him to write the subject as "being represented by a signifier for another signifier" and to write the transference as being the supposition of a convergence, in the subject-supposed-to-know, of the subject supposed to know about structure and the subject of the unconscious, supposed to unconscious knowledge. This algebra also allowed him, together with the object little *a*, which he invented from the drive objects, to write the remainder of the signifying operation, the lost being of the subject which causes his desire in his relation to the enigmatic desire of the Other. The putting into play of object little *a* in the phantasy is an attempt to make up for the radical inadequacy of language in relation to the reality of sex, to misrecognize the gap in sexual rapport. Lacan came to think that, if Freud posited the rock of castration as a limit to analysis, it was because he did not include the function of the drive object in the transference, the way the analyst is integrated as object in the fundamental phantasy of the analysand. This is precisely what the analyst works with. The reduction of the unconscious to its literality and the recognition of the "undeniability of little *a*" as void of castration, allow for the reduction of the subject-supposed-to-know to the function of object little *a*, both residue of the work and literal residue of a knowledge separated from the subject. It can then be spoken in the future anterior tense of the analyst who bore the transference: he will have been the analyst.

If this end can come about, it would be a "therapeutic" end for the transference neurosis and it would be a "didactic" end through the knowledge of structure resulting from it: a knowledge marked by a lack-of-knowledge, as the structure the subject depends on is a real one. This knowledge allows for another relation to that structure than that of the subject suffering his symptom; that one cannot "have" this knowledge allows one to use it differently than as "power". How, in this end, is the desire formed to support this operation for another subject? In which way does the act at play in this end, if it is an "analytic act", enter into the being of he who can become an agent of this discourse? It is at this point of the end of the treatment and the analytic act that Lacan placed the proposition he made to the school in 1967, concerning a new work and training mechanism, that of the *pass*.

* * *

The formalization of psychoanalytic knowledge that Lacan introduced was slow, continuous, and hesitant; far from being a conceptual systematization, it was a sometimes unsettling reinvention of the psychoanalysis Freud had invented. Like Freud, who had not hesitated to introduce concepts that shook this edifice (like narcissism, the death drive, and the mechanism of disavowal), Lacan did not shrink from the kind of revisions that could destabilize his earlier constructions (like the invention of the object little *a* and the introduction of the Borromean knot). Freud would at times address himself to correspondents, or even a fictional interlocutor, but he privileged writing; Lacan, in his constructions, addressed himself to the listeners at his seminar and he used writing to transmit the knowledge that emerged from it. In the *Acte de Fondation*, he proposed putting to the test of criticism the supposed effects of his teaching on analysands, especially his own, who had access to his seminars. The IPA, who objected to this practice, gave the training analyst the power to evaluate the level of progress of the treatment and the duty to report on it to the Training Committee; which was also not without effects on the transference. One can smile at this circularity, but it reveals the absence of a theory of training which would take into account the fact of the unconscious.

Developing the time of the subject and "positing" the unconscious in the training of the analyst not only led Lacan to break with the standardized *timing* of sessions, but also to undo the regulated linearity of the didactic *cursus* (see Nacht, Lebovici, and Diatkine (1960), who give the position of the SPP in 1960, and Shengold (1980)). Open to analysts and analysands, then to an unspecified public, his teaching already, before the foundation of the EFP, had broken down the distinction between training and research. From the "textual seminars" on, he had been inspired in his method by the lectures, both practical and scientific, given by the study directors of the École pratique des hautes études, which were open to all and whose "pupil" Lacan had been, rather than the university didactics which continued to inspire the IPA. Lacan recognized a few masters who had founded a teaching "worthy of the name": de Clérambault, Ey, hailing his thought and teaching "that makes for honour in one's lifetime and is the foundation of one's life work" (*E*, p. 124), Kojève, and Saussure. The Seminar opened up research and theoretical construction to all, but it had as its "goal", as its "practical stake", the training of analysts, and Lacan addressed himself to analysts. If he had to choose between publication and his oral teaching, his order of preference would have been: "that there first be analysts", and that there be "*some* psychoanalyst who responds to certain subjective emergencies" (*E*, p. 196).

Lacan could say that he spoke in his seminar as analysand, supervisee, and *passant*; these are not interchangeable positions, but they are positions of a subject. It is as subject that he addressed the analysts supposed to be present in the audience and supposed to incarnate a new status of the subject. He was able to write that "the way in which the most hidden truth manifests itself in the revolutions of a culture"—that is, the way of a style—was "the only training that [he could] aim to transmit to those who followed [him]" (*E*, p. 383). He could also write, modifying Buffon's formula, that style is "the man one addresses oneself to" (*E*, p. 3). What, then, is the training function of this addressee, and hence of Lacan's style? The analyst makes himself the agent, *qua* object, of discourse, but the analysand addresses him as subject supposed to know. Lacan differentiated the "public" of the seminar, which occupied for him the function of the object, a look in the name of which he was speaking, from the analysts to whom he addressed himself (Lacan, 1990a, pp. 3–4). It was a way of specifying the teaching mode he already took in 1953: instituting, "even silently", a dialogue with the listener, in a striking "symmetry" with the experience of analysis, a symmetry which therefore in teaching made the analyst an analysand (Lacan, 1976, p. 56). In his "discourse" theory, Lacan said that the teacher, when there is one, is found there where the subject is, and that he teaches as subject in order to learn, not to transmit a knowledge; the one who is taught is so only at the level of his own knowledge, of his relation as subject to this knowledge (Lacan, 2001).

In analytic discourse, the knowledge at play is unconscious; what the analysing subject learns from, the kind of knowledge with which he can make himself a teacher for the analyst, is knowledge of structure, which, being real, is a knowledge that includes a lack. Lacan thought that the Freudian object allowed a new status of the subject; it is to those supposedly new subjects that he addressed himself. This subject is new in the sense that Freud's *neues Subjekt* of the third moment of the drive is. The reading Lacan gave of the trajectory of the drive as an outline of the act makes of this subject not the one performing an act, but the one resulting from an act whose agent is the object (Lacan, 1991, p. 178). It is at that point of the act, in the very place of the "without hope" proper to the "making oneself heard" of the third moment of the drive, that Lacan could, in the end, situate his teaching. If he was able to say that his act saved him from teaching it was in so far as his teaching was operating at the junction between the analysing task and the psychoanalytic act (Lacan, 1968a, p. 47). It was as subject in training himself, but more *passant* than analysand, that he addressed himself to subjects in training, sometimes despairing of their existence.

The aim here is less to bring out the exceptional character of this teaching than to grasp in what way it makes a "case". It was a case for the EFP because it was an occasion for a choice, hence an act, for those who preferred a teaching that would say what analysis is to the conformity of a standardized view. It set a precedent when it allowed the development, beyond the person of Lacan, of how what it is that analysis teaches can be taught, in a "transmission from one subject to another". That Lacan upheld this in a position of exteriority in relation to the School was not without risk. He recognized in the *Founding Act* that his teaching could have the effect of an impasse, not on analysands, but on the work of the School, due to the "induction" it aimed at. In order that his teaching created an induction in the sense of the reasoning it designated, that is, allowing one to construct a knowledge on the basis of given elements it was necessary that everybody put something of himself as subject into it.

* * *

The admission of candidate analysts to supervision is one of the essential links in the chain of progress in the *cursus* instituted by the IPA; it is the compulsory step which gives access to all of the teaching and scientific activities, as well as to being admitted as a member authorized to practise without supervision. Even when reforms in France got rid of pre-selection, the list of trainers and the idea of training analysis, the authorization to undertake "supervised treatments", followed by the validation of that supervision, remained the prerogative of the institution, the locus of its responsibility and its guarantee; thus, the guarantee of what it gave (of itself). Supervision is the place in which the passage from analysand to the status of analyst is played out, the passage from one status to another, within the context of an institution that thinks it can identify and authorize the analyst. Can the conditions for the definition and recognition of this identity do anything other than push one's analysis, even if it is called "personal", towards this integration and this identity? Can they escape producing an "idealizing transference" that inflects the analysis towards the ideals of the institution, even if reduced to the institution of supervision?

Caring little for this institutional logic and little inclined towards this practice, Freud and Ferenczi privileged the transmission of technical advice, communicating in publications their trials, their errors and their advances. Freud's correspondence shows him to have been generous with his advice and references to his own experience, as well as sometimes judging severely the deafness of the analyst in the treatment (see his judgement of an analysis conducted by Jones [Paskaukas, 1993, pp. 483–484, 491]). The letters to Eduardo Weiss show his position as "consultant", which he accepted readily, even at times seeing both analyst and patient together, giving practical indications or a prognosis on the basis of a case presentation, sharing his experience but leaving the initiative to the inventiveness and judgement of the analyst (Weiss, 1970). Weiss put him more in the position of "casuist" than "supervisor", preferring to address himself to Federn, his old analyst, for the cases of psychoses, which Freud, according to him, declined to treat. After fifteen years of epistolary exchanges and meetings discussing fifteen or so cases, he trusted his own judgement against Freud's advice and only consulted him occasionally from then on.

Has the deregulation of the training and the suppression of the *cursus* at the EFP modified the practice of supervision? The note added to the *Founding Act* in the summer of 1964 specified that supervision "imposed itself'" as soon as a practice based itself on analytic effects, in order to protect patients, and that the School would be responsible for supervisions: they were part of the responsibility of the subject committing himself to this practice (Lacan, 1965). In the text, which specified the functioning and administration of the School, it was the only part of the training that retained the mark of the previous institution. Even if membership of the School no longer depended on it (as it did on being engaged in a work project), the title of analyst member of the school (AME) did. A resolution taken by the first directorate, in March 1965, stated that the Membership Committee would propose names of supervisors to the trainees. Balint had questioned supervision as a place of "superegoic formation" and as an initiatory transmission solidifying a group around a master, but his critique had no consequence. Even if the resolution taken by the directorate of the EFP was not followed, the practice of supervision was at that time a subject of agreement beyond any institutional split, no doubt because it encouraged the belief that analytic practice derives from a technique which could be learnt, as Eitingon wanted, from a master artisan who would accompany the first steps of the would-be analyst: no doubt because this belief sets up an Other who would be completed by his knowledge, initiator and guarantor, himself guaranteed by his inscription in the genealogical chain of transmission. The article in *Scilicet*, 6–7, which tried to establish a non-institutionalized practice of supervision, uses this metaphor of a profession which *is learnt* as one learns to walk; curiously, however, the author does not link this practice to the problematic Lacan stressed of the *gradus*, that is, the step (Lacan, 1976, p. 205). The expression "treatment referred to a third party" had a currency in the EFP, and the term "supervision" (*contrôle*), which Lacan qualified as "sinister" (*E*, p. 210), would prevail among his pupils over other formulations, the variations indicating the aporias of this practice: supervision analysis, control, supervised treatment, assisted listening, fourth analysis.

It is important to take seriously the fact that one finds in Lacan neither a theory of supervision nor a questioning of its necessity.

When the Rome congress of the EFP devoted a morning to the theme of supervision in 1974, several analysts attempted to sketch a doctrine of supervision; Lacan did not intervene. Yet, it is difficult to maintain that he would have been satisfied with uninformed practice and to conclude that its theory remained to be written, or that it is just a part of the doctrine of pure analysis. In 1966, Lacan specified that the values of supervision were to be found on the one hand in the clues about structure to be found in his teaching, and on the other in the construction, during the treatment, of "the fundamental screen of the real in the unconscious phantasy" (*E*, p. 195). The construction of the subject and the object, the "building" of the unconscious phantasy that supports desire, therefore have a supervisory value. The *Acte de Fondation* sheds light on Lacan's position on this practice, which, even though non-institutionalized, remains a "hybrid", partaking of analysis as well as medical ethics, and not without giving to the supervisor some power of recognition and guarantee.

Lacan chose to place the practice of supervision within the rubric of pure analysis, like the effects of training and teaching given by the treatment and his seminar. He brought back the necessity of supervision to a "fact" about which the *cursus* of the training did not want to know anything: that subjects in analysis are led to taking analytic responsibility in their professional practice. In that "particular case", it is necessary that the analytic effects in the practice of someone who is not an analyst are recognized by the practitioner, as much to protect the patient as himself. To speak of "analytic (-ally inspired) psychotherapy" is equivalent to a negation of the fact that analytic practice precedes for the most part the authorization of the analyst *qua* analyst, and that this does not change at all with the institutional recognition that comes from supervision. To recognize this fact and to link it as soon as it presents itself to the necessity of supervision, is to choose a non-mendacious training rather than an idealized training; it is to allow the practitioner not to shirk his function, but it requires a radical rethink of the question of authorization and the aporias of supervision. Lacan, therefore, asked himself if it would not be better, in order to avoid putting the training analysis in an impasse, to moderate, in agreement with the analysand, their practice of "analytic psychotherapy".

The beginning of a practice, whether in the institution or in a liberal "setting", is most often the staging of a wanting-to-be-an-analyst from which the desire of the analyst has not yet been filtered. Beneath the appearance of technical problems, the difficulties and obstacles encountered put in play the relation of the practising subject to his own particular unconscious knowledge and the relation to a *jouissance* not yet drained by the treatment; his relation to knowledge, to power, and to the object is thus compromised. Most of these problems concern the not-yet-analysed aspects of an ongoing treatment, even the limbo of an interrupted analysis. This was the idea behind the principles adopted by the Hungarian School: it suggested that supervision be conducted by the training analyst, side by side with the training analysis (Kovacs, 1936). It is an idea verified when supervision leads to the resumption of the analysis for which it was the unrecognized demand (Stein, 1977). That is why Lacan could maintain that the project of supervision be clarified between analyst and analysand and could himself undertake the supervision of certain analysands, or at certain moments of analysis, with a sometimes very minimal distance from the analysis itself.

Wishing to speak about the start of one's analytic practice is to realize and acknowledge that neither one's wanting-to-be-an-analyst nor the phantasy with which one authorizes oneself, nor one's acquired knowledge, are sufficient to orientate oneself in relation to the signifiers and the letter of the analysand, in handling the transference within the setting of the treatment, and embodying the place of the object from which the act can operate. But addressing oneself to a supervisor, supposed to be experienced or not, can also be a demand for recognition and authorization, a demand to be inscribed in a filiation, a network, or an institution. It depends for a large part on the type of response, and thus on the position of the supervisor, whether the authorization specific to the analytic act is neglected or not and whether the practitioner comes to believe or not that he can authorize himself by means of his supervisor.

The fate of this aporia, which reveals a demand for initiation at the heart of a procedure with technical aims, does not solely depend on the treatment that someone "supervised" can carry out, but also on the position of the one he addresses. If we were to read "pure analysis" as an anticipation of the "analytic discourse" Lacan would formulate six years later, then we could try to read what the social bond of supervision might be within this discourse. The analyst in "supervision" re the treatment he conducts speaks as a subject, putting to work not only what he understands of the text of the analysand, his locating of the knot of the transference, but also his own implicit theory. If the analyst to whom he addresses himself is not there in terms of a technical, theoretical, or clinical knowledge he "possesses", nor there as master signifier, nor in the place of the object as the analyst of the supervisee would be, then he can only be there as a subject of these types of knowledge: that supposed subject realized by the analytic discourse to which Lacan addressed himself when he supervised himself by means of his seminar. It is not only the prerogative of an analyst starting his practice to address himself to another analyst, or to some others, to illuminate his practice and account for it; it is not a form of address limited to supervision. Lacan came to think that "supervision of the act" (Lacan, 1970a, p. 18) ought to have a specific apparatus devoted to it. The reading of this act, accounting for it, the supervision of what makes a passage from one position to another within the same discourse, was entrusted to the apparatus of the *pass*.

Cartels

I – PSYCHANALYSE PURE.
   1 – Devenir analyste.
   2 – Transfert et Interprétation.
   3 – Pulsions.
   4 – Sujet et Subjectivité.
   5 – Le rêve et son interprétation.
   6 – La science des rêves.
   7 – Groupe belge.

II – PSYCHANALYSE APPLIQUEE.
   1 – Perversions.
   2 – Clinique de la Psychose (Strasbourg).
   3 – Mise en question de la psychanalyse d'enfants Problème de la débilité mentale.
   4 – Relation thérapeutique.
   5 – Psychothérapie d'enfants en groupes d'analystes.
   6 – Psychoses de l'enfant.
   7 – Le désir en psychanalyse et eu médecine d'enfants.
   8 – Cliniques psychanalytiques.
   9 – Nosoiogie psychiatrique et Institutions.
  10 – Groupe de Montpellier (Faure).
  11 – Groupe de Vaucluse.
  12 – Thérapeutique et expression artistique.
  13 – Les interactions nevrotiques.

III – RECENSEMENT DU CHAMP FREUDIEN
   1 – Theorie du discors.
   2 – Psychothérapie individuelle et institutionnelle (G T PSY).
   3 – Altérité juive.
   4 – Psychanalyse et religion.
   5 – Etudes bibliques.
   6 – Psychodrame.
   7 – Anthropologie psychanalytique

Reproduction of Cartels listed in the École freudienne de Paris directory, 1965.

CHAPTER SIX

The Apparatuses of the School

Issues of the mechanisms

Did Lacan take the risk of encouraging the wild training that Jones had so dreaded? As soon as a training is deregulated and essentially referred to "pure psychoanalysis", the necessity of the institution for a training is put into question. But the notion of school can be differentiated from the notion of institution. That is the sense of Ey's answer to Lacan's request that he join the Freudian School of Paris: "A school is formed when a master teaches freely to free students. A school is not an institution; it is not based on its officiality but on the prestige of its master" (Ey's letter to Lacan, quoted in Roudinesco, 1990, pp. 429–430). While praising the "great intellectual courage" and "immense effort" of Lacan, he discouraged him from weighing himself down with an institution. He regretted that Lacan did not break with "the adventure of lay analysis" and did not remain for the medical analysts the master that he was and that they needed. Even if he did not grasp the full measure of Lacan's attempt to renounce the position of master of truth by incorporating the problematic of the desire of the analyst into the institution, Ey saw very well that the stake of this institution was the setting up of analysis as a lay practice.

One might think that the institution serves to announce one's setting up in the profession, something which remains clandestine in the IPA unless authorized by one's Society. One might think that it serves to retroactively confer recognition on a prior training and to constitute a clientele through plugging into a network of power and influence in which supervision can take on a decisive function for each of the participants. One might think that it offers to analysts supposedly already trained the occasion to train further, following their theoretical options, that is, to the theorizing that conforms to the small part of subjectivity proper to each. Last, one could attribute to it the task of sustaining an *orthè doxa* against which everyone can test the phantasmatic elucubrations with which they would rationalize the enigma of their desire and the way it is put to work in their practice. The question of doctrine and its transmission was central to Freud's institutional initiative prior to any notion of training and qualification. In creating an institution that was solid enough to shelter the doctrinal kernel, he left himself the liberty to continue inventing analysis. But he also took the risk that the orthodox censors he had instituted would ignore the revisions he might introduce. Lacan and some others with him thought that the foundation of the School found its guarantee in a teaching devoted to redeveloping analytic doctrine by getting as close as possible to its object. It was a way of suggesting that a training appropriate to the particularity of lay analysis might require a very different relation to doctrine and to the *"praxis* of theory" than the one induced by the institution of an orthodoxy or the reference to a master (of truth or knowledge).

A wild training was no more agreeable to Lacan than to Freud; but "regular transmission", governed by the second fundamental rule, seemed to him more in keeping with analytic rigour than a regulated transmission. Because of the discipline of work and thought it presupposes, his "liberal" reference of 1953 actually went against free enterprise, something that derives in the final analysis from the ego. It is doubtless not surprising that the principle he formulated in 1967—"an analyst only authorises himself from himself"—lent itself to ambiguity as much as his reference to the liberal arts did. This principle, which demands rigour from both the subject and the institution, has been used to authorize the self-authorization of the liberal "setting up practice". The misunderstanding is both radical and simple: understood as a "oneself authorizing oneself", the principle would read in the first person: "I myself authorize myself " ("we authorize ourselves"). Recognition would then be equivalent to "you yourself authorize yourself". But Lacan's principle, which concerns the absent part of the subject, rigorously contradicts these formulations and can only be said in the third person. It involves a different requirement from the analytic community and the institution, which Lacan would formulate in 1974, specifying that the analyst authorizes himself from himself and from "some others". Not from some ones. The formulation of this principle, in 1967, responded in a certain sense to the error of Nacht, which had led to the split in 1953. It is important to note that Lacan only articulated it at the moment that he produced the "apparatus" designed to treat, by renewing it, the question left latent during the foundation of the School—the question of recognition and qualification.

Despite the Hegelian idea which, in the 1950s, allowed the substitution of the "training oneself" of the *Bildung* of the classical age, for the "one trains" of the artisanal model, and despite the radical critique of the organization of the IPA, Lacan did not simply take "a negative path" when it came to the institution. The teaching and the study days always took account of the scientific, medical, and psychiatric context. With the diffusion of the work in the *Lettres de l'École*, several journals participated in the mechanism of training, distributed over the three sections in the manner of a "musical training": *L'Inconscient, Scilicet, L'Ordinaire du psychanalyste, Ornicar?*. But Lacan was familiar with what happens to spontaneous institutions, like the one Freud had allowed to develop, first failing to theorize itself, second for lack of a theory (and hence an imaginary) capable of sustaining another mode of organizing itself. The School training is, therefore, also a way of responding to the spontaneous institution, almost in the sense of a "military training" (Lacan spoke of an "operational base") obeying a strategy. Lacan, in effect, had attempted to forge a social bond between analysts *and* analytic discourse. He saw it as a condition for letting analytic training remain within the field of Freud's discovery, as other discourses barred access to this (Lacan, 1973, p. 10).

The spontaneous institution, however powerfully organized and historically determined, obeys the psychology of groups which

Freud analysed in *Massenpsychologie und Ichanalyse* (Freud, 1921c, pp. 67–145). It allows disparate elements to hold together, united by one common attribute: an identity—a professional identity, but also a reference to a founder can take on this function. The illusory character of this link in no way invalidates its efficacy, this latter deriving in large part from the "confusion in a single point, of the signifier of the ideal in which the subject locates himself with the 'a', that is, the localization in that point of *jouissance*" (Lacan, 1991, p. 257). It is a way of dealing with number. The "extra" trait (a leader, incarnated or not, a doctrine, the "name of one", the voice of a dead person) that sustains the identification of each with the collective allows one to keep adding new elements to the others indefinitely. There is no numerical limit to this expansion, which contains an indefinite number of entities and which aims to base its power on numbers. The spontaneous institution is coherent with the dominant social bond in which the subject is instituted by a master signifier, which divides him certainly, but in which this division is phantasmatically denied, giving the subject hope of being completed by the object of his desire and thus rejoin the "self'" he was separated from. Transference links do not contradict this movement as they proceed by identification and the attribution of an agalmatic object to the analyst. The history of analytic institutions repeatedly illustrates the reciprocal collusion of spontaneous institutions and transference links, showing how the incidence of these links on the group can, inversely, lead treatments and theory into an impasse, bar access to Freud's discovery, and prevent the knowledge of structure at work in the analytic act from being constructed.

In some respects, the mechanism of the EFP revived the spirit of the first analytic societies, but, it also inherited the history of the analytic movement and the difficult problems to which the IPA had given a standard response: how to treat numbers and proper names, qualification and recognition (mutual and social), the relation of the subject and his theorizing to doctrine, the relations between power and authority, and the incidence of the transference on these issues. The training of the analyst in the treatment itself depends on the modalities of the institutional response to these questions. Lacan founded, in the School, the hope of a community of work and experience, which his "doctrinal apparatus" tried to orientate. Yet, in relation to this apparatus, the School could only be a "remainder", a remainder he could not predict beforehand. In effect, doctrine is not sufficient to constitute a community "of work and critique" which would not lead to either the spontaneous institution or the ghettoization produced by scientific and social extraterritoriality. Some desire is required, articulated differently by analytic discourse, as well as specific mechanisms more suited to the social bond of analysis, capable of creating a social bond with other analysts, and of responding differently to the difficulties inherited from analytic history.

In order to grasp the importance of the two mechanisms of work and training proposed by Lacan, it could be useful to dwell on this notion of an apparatus (*dispositif*). Lacan used this term to speak of the "arranged experience" (*experience disposé*) of the treatment. He saw in it, more than in the invention of the unconscious, the true creation of Freud, in so far as it is an "apparatus the real of which touches the real" (Lacan, 1975a, p. 6). A number of his pupils extended the use of the term to the cartel, to the procedure of the *pass*, patient presentations, and to procedures of working on clinical practice. But it is also a notion conceptualized by Foucault in order to analyse the mutual determination of the relations between knowledge and power, the "strategies of power relations which underlie different types of knowledge" (Foucault, 1997).

As a heterogeneous network of institutions, scientific, philosophical, or moral statements, legal or rule-related decisions and administrative practices, an apparatus is, according to him, a "formation" which derives from a strategy. Not necessarily attributable to a person and tied to the objective that is its organizing matrix, it is linked to the limits of knowledge: thus, the apparatus of incarceration (for madness or delinquency), of alliances, of fixing the cost of manual labour, of sexuality. In the strategy he attributed to the apparatus of sexuality of getting one to confess sex and getting sex to profess the truth of the human being, Foucault highlighted the way knowledge and power presuppose and capture each other. Later, following a theoretical "crisis", he would isolate the agency of the subject, differentiating the subjectivization produced by the apparatus and which allows one to escape it (resistance, flight, subversion, action, invention) from the simple subordination produced by the reciprocal play of power and knowledge. This subjectivization does not occur without dividing the subject in his relation to himself.

Contemporary with the apparatuses that Foucault studied, a social apparatus of training was formed; professional training was one of its effects, among others (and hence the generalization of schooling and the pedagogic discourse accompanying it). The IPA subordinated the training of analysts to it, hoping to resolve the problems posed by the transmission of analysis and the recognition of a growing number of analysts, who were training psychotherapy professionals. Freud had tried to resist this kind of response, but encountered a limit of knowledge (the aetiology of psychosis) and the capture of analytic knowledge by the medical establishment; in the end, he included "psychoanalysing" in his list of "impossible professions". Lacan tried to subvert this response of the IPA by thinking of the training of the analyst in as close a conjunction as possible with the subject that can result from the "culture" of the formations of the unconscious. His project was to show how this culture has to take account not only of the subject as effect of language, but also of the object that causes unconscious desire.

Where the phantasy includes the object as a possible complement of the subject, fixing desire and guiding it into the path of misrecognition, the treatment brings out the impossibility of this complementarity: the object is lost, and being is lacking to image and text. As a time and space for this analysis is an apparatus: it is not without knowledge, even if this knowledge is "in reserve", or without "direction", even if devoid of mastery. The apparatus can confront the subject with the impossibility at the root of the human condition because it is itself structured by this impossibility. Lacan first approached this by means of the "subjective disparity" which blocks intersubjectivity within the transference. By means of the logic of the subject and the elucidation of the object little a, he could specify how the analyst should sustain the mistake of the appeal to the subject supposed to know, enlist its presence in order to operate with an object raised to the level of *"semblant"*, and cause the desire of the subject *against* the phantasy in which the analysand has placed it. This gives the real of the apparatus with which the analyst must guide himself, case by case, in order to set the times of the treatment (length of the face-to-face work and passage to the couch, frequency and scansion of sessions, right moments to interpret), but also his attitude to the payment of sessions. Can one profess, and thus declare publicly, an act which "forces the phantasy" and uncovers the intolerable aspect of the seeming which the economy of enjoyment is based on, giving value and meaning to everything that matters in the world? There, doubtlessly, lies the impossible side of the "profession". Yet, the analyst cannot evade this impossibility. The social bond, whose agent he becomes in so far as he has been its effect, cannot divorce itself from the other social bonds; he participates, after all, in the synchrony of discourses. But neither can he shelter within a profession which is more in keeping with the dominant social bond (medicine or psychotherapy), or content himself with declaring his name and revenue.

To carry out an operation that requires, at its end, not only the suspension of the hypothesis it is based on (the subject of the unconscious), but also the collapse of its agent (the subject supposed to know that makes the transference), requires an atheism of method more than of opinion or conviction. This atheism should also be applied to theory as well as to our relation to it, to the subject supposed to know that is latent to it as much as to the figure of master of the occult, which threatens to turn non-knowing into mystagogics. That is probably the real issue of lay analysis. To make a profession out of the (little) knowledge and (little) power that the real of structure leaves us in order to do something with it, and perhaps determine it, cannot be done on one's own. The treatment invites us to render unconscious knowledge subjective by supposing a subject to it, close to the belief in a God or a master who would know the truth of being and had the power of our salvation. In this closeness, the subject is confronted with the enjoyment supposed to this Other but also expected from him. Reducing unconscious knowledge to its literality and producing the object little *a* through the emptying out of the *jouissance* attached to the drive objects with which he imagines himself, is the business of analysis, allowing the handling of the object and use of one signifier for another, in the very place of subjective division. The little bit of knowledge thus constructed in the treatment with the bringing together of these two literalities allows one to subjectivize the long path by which Freud, Lacan, and others found their way in this structure. It no doubt requires a double movement of subjectivization and objectivization of this knowledge in order to recognize it in others. In different ways and at different times, the apparatuses of the cartel and the *pass* allow the association with others, which is a precondition for it.

The Cartel

Freud had made it a rule at the Wednesday Society that everyone should speak. In January 1954, Lacan reminded the participants in his seminar that the tradition of "textual seminars" requires that each give his utmost in order to contribute to the "common task". At the end of the session, rather like a "tutor", he proposed to Mannoni and Anzieu to collaborate to study the notion of resistance in the technical writings of Freud, and he proposed the same project to Perrier and Granoff (Lacan, 1990a, p. 18). He added: "We shall see how we will proceed. We will let ourselves be guided by the experience itself". Ten years later, no doubt instructed by experience, he proposed another formula for work in the School: the principle of a "sustained elaboration" in a small group of three to five people "PLUS ONE charged with the selection, the discussion, and the fate reserved for the work of each". The note added to the *Acte de Fondation* gives the name, kept in reserve, of this group: the cartel. It is a word referring to the paper which supports writing (*cartello, charta, kartès*), to the public (the cartello artists painted signs), but also to a structure of association, whether political, economic, or artistic. The "cartel" of Dullin, Jouvet, Baty, and Pitoëff, set up in 1927 for "professional esteem and mutual respect", aimed to encourage an effort of research and creation by joining the particularity of each and the freedom to choose themes for artistic rather than commercial reasons (Scarpalezou, 1995).

Though the cartel carried these meanings, it also evoked the experience of Bion and Rickman in the England of 1940; it was an experience which was decisive for Bion's clinical research and his institutional positions, but was to lead Rickman astray in his inquiry into the analysts who had collaborated with the *Goering-Institut*. Lacan, in 1945, was enthusiastic about the civilizing work of these two analysts who managed to find "in the very impasse of a situation the vital force of intervention". By organizing the rejects of the army draft into small leaderless groups, they managed to rethink the group solidarity of an aggregate of misfits who had problems at the level of identification and highlighted the "reference of the individual to each of the others" in which he himself, at the end of the war, located the fundamental requirement for a logic of the collective (Lacan, 1947, 1986). Addressing himself to "those for whom the synthesis of the particular and the universal has concrete political meaning", he staged a "return to logic" which would disconcert those minds "whose training was only habit". He tried first to determine pure difference by allowing the play of the "position by-three-and-one" in the logic of suspicion that is the basis of the "absolute notion of difference".

In the logic of the subject worked out in "Le temps logique", "the truth for all depends on the rigour of each" (Lacan, 2006e, p. 173). To the "generality", which contains an indefinite number of individuals, unified and identified by a judgement of attribution (S is P by virtue of its identification to a common ideal), Lacan opposed the "collectivity" formed by the mutual relations of a defined number of subjects. In the sophism of the prisoners three are necessary in order to produce each one as a subject of pure logic. The prisoner's release, in haste, only comes about when each one only functions in the ternary as the object little *a* that he *is* in the eyes of the others. The separation from this object, before it is too late, allows a subjective affirmation and *makes* the collective (*tres faciunt collegium*), a collective formed around an empty place.

It is with this logic that one should approach the structure of the work apparatus that Lacan proposed in order to contribute, together with the treatment, to the formation of the subject and the knowledge that can help an analyst. Because of a limit on both the number of participants and the duration of the work, a cartel allows the dimension of haste to operate that is constitutive of a subject in relation to the object and the Other. It is not the aim of the cartel to constitute, as a "whole", some "ones" united around a master or a tutor who would be the "One-more" charged with enforcing a master's knowledge, or to have produced, in a more hysterical manner, a knowledge for a master. If the cartel were only a group without a leader, nothing would guarantee that the natural inclination to set one up would not operate. To identify the function of "plus-one" in a random but real person tends rather to maintain active for each the question of the mode of identification with the collective. Lacan formulated it thus: if one has to identify with the group, which point of identification allows one not to make a "mob"? If he is there to represent an empty place, that of the lack-of-knowledge, the "plus-one" can allow each person to situate the relevant knowledge in the place from which it operates in the discourse of the analyst, the place of truth. In the encounters with texts or the knowledge of others that speak to him, the subject can tie the knowledge he constructs, or has constructed, in the treatment, with his unconscious knowledge and the knowledge that Freud, Lacan, and others have developed, as well as with the clinical knowledge learnt from treatments.

This position of the subject, working with a few other subjects, is one of the happiest realizations of the "transmission from subject to subject" in which Lacan situated the "work transference". No doubt it is because it forms a *hapax* that he never developed into a concept that this expression has curiously served to name the displacement of transference links from the treatment to the institution. Understanding this as a transference of transference is partly due to the fact that such links are present in an institution in which analysts and analysands mingle. But this sliding of meaning also legitimizes the confusion, in one person, of analyst, master teacher and head of a group. It is a confusion that has primarily concerned the place given to Lacan—accepted by him?—and continues to be relevant to some "ones", with a theory of "remainders of transference" sometimes being used to justify a politics of transference. The resistance to the apparatus of the cartel is perhaps grounded in this. In 1975, Lacan felt that there had perhaps not yet been a realization of a cartel in the School and that it had therefore not yet begun to function as such.

The cartel can show the uniqueness of the knowledge that is formed in analysis, in relation to other discourses or theoretical practices. With its "plus-one", it is not just a working group or the tutoring that some university traditions have instituted so that the teacher is not the only one taught by what he is trying to transmit. There is an ethic pertaining to the university discourse that analysts should not ignore in their attempts to set up a specific theoretical practice. It is not certain that the cartel is enough to bring the kind of historical and critical information that makes the discipline of university teaching and research what it is. There would, therefore, be reason to rejoice if an analytical institute made a place for this theoretical practice in its teachings and if the university and research bodies made a place for analysis (cf. Roudinesco, 1990, pp. 223–226, 547–579 for the historical references to this question). To feel alarmed or to ignore it would be equivalent to putting the discourse of the analyst, wrongly, in a position of exception within the synchrony of discourses. But this tendency is also linked to the impasses that would result from wanting to train analysts at the university. The training of analysts deriving from the practice of "pure analysis", that is, from the culture of the unconscious, cannot take place there; teaching, as well as research, would be divorced from a practice that clinical courses cannot replace. The operative knowledge that matters here is the one tying the unconscious knowledge of the subject to the knowledge of doctrine and of the clinic. It is from this knotting that those discoveries can emerge that research is supposed to aim for and that conducting the treatment sometimes necessitates.

The other difficulty derives, in a necessary and non-contingent way, from the fact that the transference relation, the supposition of knowledge and of the subject, which are always brought into play by a teaching relationship and the transmission of a theory, cannot be analysed in a university setting. Yet, there is no training of an analyst without analysis of the transference and its de-supposition. Moreover, the inclination of the discourse of the university is to amass knowledge into a "Summa" and to reduce the role of research, which, in its scientific dimension, derives rather from hysterical discourse. It is an inclination which risks systematizing knowledge and runs counter to the critical approach, even contributing to dogmatism. The most dangerous systematization of analytic knowledge is the one that would reduce it to just another variant of psychological knowledge. At best, but perhaps not for the best, it would be the Berlin model, a model which seems to carry within it the mark of Abraham's fascination for the university. Even if he supported, and not without ambivalence, the university adventure of Vincennes, Lacan opted to guide himself with the teaching of the study directors of a non-university institution, the École Pratique des Hautes Études. It would, however, be unjust not to acknowledge the discipline of criticism set at the heart of the Freudian School of Paris. If not sufficient to give it its tools, the work of the cartels nonetheless, when effective, allows one to grasp its necessity; it is then situated within the old tradition, taken up by Lacan, of "textual seminars".

Transmitting to the general public is one of the possible outcomes of cartel work, in the form of a communication, a text whose mode of distribution can vary and is sometimes a publication. Writing, and the reading it implies, is one of the paths of training, partaking of the discipline of the letter that the analyst must master for the practice of reading and writing in the treatment itself. It was a decisive step in the training for those first analysts who participated in the journals that Freud tirelessly supported. In this context, we ought to stop and look at Lacan's curious project with *Scilicet* (we will elaborate on this question in an article to be published in the journal *Essaim*). Its formula was borrowed from the collective enterprise of the mathematicians from the Nicolas Bourbaki group, yet it was quite different: no collective editorial, no strict anonymity, since a list of names took responsibility for the whole publication, and, last but not least, Lacan's proper name in the position of exception in which the exclusion of 1963 had put him. Lacan linked this to training, giving the non-identification of the author in *Scilicet* as a "proof of training" (Lacan, 1970b, p. 4). That he saw it as a proof of training does not make it one of its paths. That is clear from Lacan's intervention on the cartel in April 1975, during the study days organized by the EFP around the work and functioning of cartels.

Concluding the study days, Lacan stated that analysis cannot hold together analysts the way mathematics allows mathematicians to form a working community. It is a remark that was contemporary with his step in moving from writing mathemes to writing knots, one he himself qualified as "failed *mathesis*". It is a step that allows one to specify the point of a cartel. Lacan must have recognized that there is no set of the Symbolic, Imaginary, and Real, but that they hold together when knotted around a hole. This knotting, in which each dimension determines a mode of naming, can shed light on the way certain "ones", who are far from whole, and heterogeneous in their singular relation to analysis, can hold together. Lacan maintained on that day that if they can work together on a knowledge that was not easily shared, it is only on condition that each person in a cartel bear his name.

The very particular signifier of the proper name partakes, on one side, of the pure dimension of the letter, but it also involves the voice pronouncing it, calling it. A remainder of naming, having no other signification than a string of phonemes and letters, it evokes with each inscription or utterance the signifier which is lacking in the place of the Other to name the subject as a speaking being. A neurotic does not bear his name; he is rather bothered by the way the proper name is taken up into the imaginary of a name which would carry the ego; his fascination for the "name of One", in which La Boétie recognized the principle of voluntary servitude, makes of him a "Name-less" one haunted by the name. If the "plus-one", on whose name three or four people agreed, is happy to bear his name without attributing any other signification to it than its pure literality, it can allow himself and a few others to work together and advance in a knowledge that is never "completely it"; advance by carving out the place of their enunciation in it.

A cartel brings otherness into play. It contains differing, time-bound relations to knowledge that depend on the moment in treatment and practice in which each person finds himself; prior studies and the relations they determine to the work of culture, and even practices themselves, are also diverse; even if a text or clinical or theoretical question is the common theme, what motivates each person in his relation to psychoanalysis remains singular. This heterogeneity contributes to reopen the field of the unconscious that, by its nature, tends to close, and to shape the construction of knowledge in it. It creates, in a different way from the treatment, a "that is not quite it". In this sense, the cartel partakes of that "path of training" which Lacan hoped to transmit and which derived from his style of work "in progress'. In 1975, he defined for the students of Columbia University how, from the style of his youth ("that is not quite it"), he forged a style which "tried to capture very closely what "is very much it" (Lacan, 1976, p. 48). Like his development, it was a style "in progress", which required successive formalizations and writings and which created the passage from mathemes to knots. Lacan introduced the knot in 1972, in order to write the formula of love: "I am asking you to refuse what I am offering you because it is not it". In the place of the impossible, of which the "that is not it" is the index, he would place in the knot the object little *a*.

If Lacan's formalization gives access to the theory of object little *a*, the formation of this object depends on the treatment. If the apparatus of the cartel works very closely with the "that is not quite it", the apparatus of the *pass* confronts analysts with the necessity of getting close to what is "very much it" by having to recognize whether this object causes the desire of the analyst.

The Pass

A little before the end of her training days in Vienna, Freud spoke with Lou Andreas-Salomé about the reasons that informed her decision to devote herself to analysis. She spoke of the importance of a "science in the making", which always brings one back to a beginning, and her debt in relation to an experience of the unconscious which, whether joyous or tormenting, is an experience of our real being (Andreas-Salomé, 1991, pp. 89–90; Pfeiffer, 1966, pp. 56–57, 181). Later, she would write to him to say that this beginning was the act at play at the beginning of any "psychoanalysing", first of all for Freud himself. Neither of them could have imagined that an analyst would develop the logic of this act and would aim to shape training by means of this logic. Only Ferenczi had the intuition that a training institution could be based on analyses brought to completion; we have seen that Freud preferred instead the solution of a Secret Committee proposed by Jones. Lacan was ignorant of this detail from the beginnings of the history of the IPA, when he proposed to his school to guide itself with the simple fact of "psychoanalysing", with this act to which an analysis can lead at its ending. And he proposed a mechanism for it.

In this complex apparatus, a *passant* speaks separately to two *passeurs* about the circumstances of this act, of the step [*pas*] in the treatment that made him pass from the path of analysis to the position of analyst. It is a step made alone, without even the help of the phantasy that might have sustained his desire to be an analyst; it is a step he might have to take again, just as alone, in each treatment. At the end of these conversations, each *passeur* testifies before a jury about what he has heard. The result of the jury's work on these testimonies, as a function of what reaches them or not via the *passeurs* of what is spoken about the act, is that the jury then qualifies the *passant* or not as Analyst of the School. There is, thus, no direct contact with the *passant*, whose speech only reaches the jury by means of the voice of the *passeurs*, in camera. The *passeur*, even if selected at random, is not anybody; he is designated by his analyst for being, in the straits of his analysis, in that moment (*pas*) that the *passant*, who has already passed that stage, speaks to him about. The *passeur* is in that *pass* to the point of being its truth; this is a necessary condition for an account of this moment to be heard. It is not a sufficient condition: the *passeur* has to be able to be in a relation to "some others", who allow him to recognize other unconscious knowledges.

Lacan could joke, in the autumn of 1968, that this was his way of "reforming" exams, that procedure in which one only says what one supposes the examiner wants to hear. He might also have been surprised at the opposition his *Proposition* provoked among his close companions: it was only supposed to change by a hair's breadth "the demand for analysis for the purpose of training" (Lacan, 1970a, p. 24, 1970c, p. 160). The very complexity of the apparatus shows that the issues at stake were not insignificant. If the apparatus of the treatment makes the unconscious of the Freudian hypothesis exist (an unconscious which implies that one listen to it), the apparatus of the *pass* makes exist the passage from the path of analysis to the act that establishes the analyst. For the act implies that one read it in order to return to the subject from the point of misrecognition that structures it. An analyst might desire to know what it is that produces the *Verleugnung* of the act, what of the real at play in this act produces its misrecognition. Lacan thought that this *Verleugnung*, which makes for the abyss of the act, was at the root of the malaise of analytic societies. He therefore proposed to the analyst who so desired to take the second "step", the one that would make the first exist, the second turn which seals the first, by trying to read this act. The apparatus of the *pass* thus also allows for the desire of the analyst to exist, in the dimension, new for the subject, of a desire to know correlated to a few others and not only to the Other. One can perhaps now understand that it was this apparatus, together with that of the cartel, that was to make the School exist, that this was the second time of its foundation, one which is always present in any culture of foundation.

The apparatus of the *pass* also raises theoretical and clinical issues. The "arranged experience" it introduces indeed sheds light on the conditions of the moment of the *pass*: its relation to the end of the treatment and the construction of the object little *a*, the desire of the analyst formed in it, the vicissitude of the drive and the phantasy in this desire. We will content ourselves with evoking them, for the paths we had to take in order to frame the question of the training of the analyst has left little space for the experience of the *pass* and its mechanism, the study of which we will reserve for a later work. In order to approach the "fragility" of the *Proposition* we will limit our discussion to the point where Lacan intended to renew, and not abandon, a major element of the training practice of the IPA: the qualification of the analyst and the role selection plays in it. He said it in a somewhat provocative manner in December 1969 to the students of Vincennes and the analysts present at the "Impromptu" (Lacan, *Analyticon*, in 2007, p. 197). Recommending them to read a recent issue of *Études freudiennes*, he praised an article in which a member of the SPP criticized the analytic institution (Donnet, 1969). In it, he recognized his own position, specifying that he himself had drawn the conclusions of the impasse that was "masterfully exposed" in the article. He regretted that no note indicated that "in some place there is an extremist who tried to turn this into a proposition which gives new meaning to analytic selection". In 1973, in Montpellier, he was even clearer about his wish for "a different style of recruitment", which would break with the laws of competition at work in most human groups as well as with the reduction of knowledge to a commodity (Lacan, 1977). To grasp the new meaning Lacan gave to selection, it is useful to return to this traditional practice. In doing so, we have to remember that the failure of his attempt, which he recognized, and the fact that it remains subject to the trials of new experiences, no longer allow us to look down on the difficulties encountered by the IPA with respect to qualification and selection.

The communication Goodman gave during the Broadway symposium of 1980 was informed by thirty years of previous debate (Goodman, 1982). The criteria and procedures of selection had been so criticized, and were still the source of such discontent and malaise, that Goodman asked, along with others, if one ought not simply to get rid of them. Yet, the fact remained that, in spite of all the critiques, no one had abandoned these procedures; even if reduced to the final admission into a Society, the qualifications at play in this admission acted retroactively on the training. Before even considering the methods, procedures, and criteria, the first question relates to the right moment: does one need a pre-selection, or can this function be exercised by the analysis itself, giving the possibility and courage to correct an error of orientation? The earlier and more prudently one selects (in fact, on a medical basis) the more "good" analysts one risks losing. If there had to be "pre-selection" Goodman, therefore, pleaded for reduced requirements, giving a chance to analysis and space for a wager. From a list of mostly general predictive qualities and contraindications that he extracted from a compilation of articles, we retain the following: a "sustained desire to understand the mind", unanimity in excluding psychosis, as well as psychopathy and normality, an ongoing debate on whether perversion disqualifies one or not, and the shared recognition that neurosis was a good indication for a candidate to take the risk of training. The method of interview with a candidate was also unanimously agreed on. The thorny question remained that of the selectors and the theoretical and political conflicts that crystallized in this practice: who is selecting whom? And according to which wants? The discussion shed light on the most common causes for the difficulties recurrent in selection: loss of tradition for the sake of the will to modernize and democratize analysis, power struggles using networks of transferential influence in which "identification to the image of the analyst" operated, and narcissism of the trainers blinding them to their own candidates. The seriousness of the malaise stemmed from the main issue, clearly stated by Goodman, in the practice of selection: the qualification it introduces plays a crucial role in the future of analysis, since it chooses those who will embody the profession in the future, those on whom will depend whether the emphasis is put on therapeutics or research. The ideal would be to produce analysts "capable of combining to the utmost the academic with the professional".

Goodman's paper was a sign of a movement of critical reflection within the IPA, which, in some Societies, especially in France, had modified the standard training. Yet, over and above the institutional variants, the analysis that Lacan made in 1956 of the malaise of the societies has lost none of its cutting edge (Lacan, 2006k). He had written that *Sufficiency* was the "sole grade of the analytic hierarchy" and maintained ironically that, contrary to appearances (gradation in the hierarchy between categories of members), it allowed the Society to be a democratic entity (*E*, p. 397). Recognized and chosen as conformist, each analyst was a master and satisfied with being recognized as an analyst. The sufficiency would come from the mode of imaginary reproduction which, in the treatment and supervision, transmitted it. This would come in turn from a training in which authorization was received in initiatory fashion from an Other whose authority was founded, by means of the same mode of transmission, on the authority distributed by Freud with his Secret Committee. We could make the hypothesis that analysts began to push transmission into the imaginary of a "fac-simile" rather than a symbolic genealogy, when, in 1927, during the debate on lay analysis, they rejected the doctrinal authority of Freud.

In 1967, Lacan formulated the corollary of this *Sufficiency*: the misrecognition of the real at play in experience, that real which forms the analyst. He maintained that the malaise of the analytic societies derived from this misrecognition, which sufficiency introduces and takes comfort from. He therefore aimed to bring, with his *Proposition*, a solution to the problems of the societies by giving the School the means of orienting itself by means of the real rather than the ideal, to take account of the real in the training. It was a Freudian position in the sense that Freud asked of an analyst that he recognize reality. Lacan was not interested in selecting and qualifying an ideal analyst; rather, he instituted an open School training, stating that an analyst only authorized himself from himself, and proposing to recognize retroactively the relation of the analyst to the training dispensed by the School. This implies that if one follows the principle of self-authorization while tying *Sufficiency* to misrecognition of the real operating in the act which founds authorization, then the analyst should have the possibility and the means to recognize this real. It is important that one leaves him the choice, since experience shows he might prefer not to know. A different apparatus from the treatment is required, as this specific dimension of training includes the fall of the subject supposed to know, which created the transference and which can no longer be an addressee. Lacan judged that the structure of the act would require an indirect apparatus for which supervision was not suitable. Addressing some others in the *pass* had the additional benefit of allowing a knotting, controlled yet contingent, of the privacy of experience to the logic of the collective.

In its forms of recognition, the School responds to the orientation that analysts give to their practice and their interest in the experience of the School. It qualifies them according to this orientation and their relation to the training. Reversing traditional selection, which chooses the candidate (but also the analyst, the trainer, the supervisor, and the selector), the School thus recognises the modalities of the choices that the analyst made, choices that are significant re his relation to analysis. Hence, the School qualifies certain analysts as an Analyst Member of the School (AME), others as Analysts of the School (AE), and others can declare their practice without being qualified by the School. This decision, which distinguished, *within* the qualification, the hierarchy from the *gradus*, was affirmed in the written version of the *Proposition* in 1968, but it was only in 1974 that it was formulated as a logical question during a session of the seminar, *Les non dupes errent*, which was contemporary with the proposition that Lacan made to three Italian analysts of forming a school purely based on the nomination of AE. This principle of double qualification only emerged slowly, not without encountering contradictions in its modalities of application, in particular concerning the role of juries and the process of passing from one title to another. These hesitations contributed to the failure of the experience, as political calculations and sedimentary remains of the traditional selection procedure submerged the logical principle of the functioning of the *pass*.

That is why it is important to focus on the distinction Lacan made between hierarchy and *gradus* after he had pointed out that his *Proposition* did not do away with hierarchy. It is generally understood that by hierarchy Lacan referred to the positions of power within the institution, themselves linked to administrative functions, to the aura of a teacher, to the authority and performance that are reinforced by a reinstallation of the transference within the group. That would have been, in the EFP, a throwback to the IPA responsible for Lacan's first attribution of titles. From the moment the EFP was founded, Lacan, who was a trainer in the SPP and the SFP and in a position of founder, had instituted and attributed the new titles of AE and AME. Even if the nine title-holders of the SFP only made up a third of the first AE named by him (with seven associates, six trainees, and two pupils) the title of AE was inherited from the tradition of IPA titles and risked creating if not a list at least a body of trainers. And indeed, this happened at the same time that Lacan said that a trainer is only such in the future anterior, in relation to a treatment that had trained an analyst. The hierarchy he spoke of in 1956 was not this one; it was not homologous to the *Beatitudes* but to the *Sufficiency* common to all three membership categories. He did not mean to eliminate hierarchy with his proposition, but to make a break with it by inventing a procedure of qualification for the AE that would transform the title of AE instituted in 1964 (Lacan, 1977, p. 119). It is generally understood that this transformation did not institute a hierarchy between the two titles, even if the AME became the first step in the *gradus*. We propose another reading of the place of the AME.

If one can credit Lacan with not ignoring the archaic use of a term, especially when linked with a Latin one, it becomes important to grasp the distinction he introduced (Le Brun, 2000). The notion of hierarchy, which is not classical in Greek, had a great success in ecclesiastics, at the limits of theology and the social organization of the church. Designating an order determined by its beginning (*archè*) but also by its command (*arche*), both of which were sacred (*hieros*), the term was used, inspired by the Pseudo Dionysos, to think the articulation and the transmission of the order, the épistémè, and the activity of the institution. From the seventeenth century on, the administrative significance of the term drew on its repressed sacredness. Opposed to *cursus*, the *gradus* is the rung, the step, the step one takes, in the most concrete sense, a meaning found again in *passus*; but *gradus* is ambiguous because of the modern use of the term grade. In medieval Latin, the *gradus* was, like the *pass*, a maritime term designating the passage at the entrance to a port, in particular, the meeting point in an estuary between the waters of the river and the sea. The anachronistic usage of these two terms was the way Lacan found to say something new about the old and to propose something new in relation to knowledge, to the other and the institution, to the act.

Beyond the problems of pre-selection, which, after all, one could reduce or get rid of, the qualifying selection in the IPA is based on a transmission by the analyst and by the supervisor(s). This is the hierarchy, a transmission which goes back to a beginning all the more sacred for being secret, as Balint sensed in 1947, a chain linked to a principle of initiation. It is a hierarchy in which, more obviously than in other institutions, the administrative signification (and function) and the ancient religious signification that the subject supposed to know inherits are confused. It may involve the imaginary reproduction we find in the identification with the analyst or a symbolic filiation. It puts the transmission of the phallus into play. Even if Lacan qualified the bringing back of the transference in the kind of co-opting that is based on this transmission within the *hierarchia* as a "relapse", he did not reject it, but, by adding the rule of the *gradus*, the basis of the hierarchy found itself transformed, as did the title of AME introduced in 1964. As indicated by the placing on the graph of desire of the everyday-analyst, the *passeur*, the AE, and the AME, there is a retroactive effect on the AME not only from the everyday-analyst taught by Lacan, but from the AE who, also in the *pass*, is confronted with the lack of guarantee in the Other, and aims to turn into knowledge what of the object cannot be transmitted. For the imaginary reference to the hierarchy in the analytic societies, one could substitute the symbolic reference of genealogy. The AME derives from a hierarchy, that is, from a different order than the step the *passant* takes in renewing, within the apparatus of the *pass*, the step taken in analysis, making it exist in this repetition. There is, in effect, no hierarchy between these two modes of situating oneself in relation to the principle that an analyst only authorizes himself from himself. On the basis of this principle, there remains a choice of how to situate oneself in relation to authorization, to the act and the analytic community. The possibility, which seems to have haunted and petrified the admission jury, that an AME would become an AE because one of his analysands might be nominated as an AE, is contradictory with respect to the distinction made by Lacan: it introduces the genealogical principle of "hierarchy" within the *gradus*. As resistance to Lacan's invention, this possibility points to something unthought in the *Proposition*.

The qualification AME was understood to give to the "outside world" an assurance of professional capacity, the guarantee of a "sufficient" training (one can see here a nod in the direction of "sufficiencies") on the part of an analyst who had "passed the test" given by an admission jury, which was also charged, in 1964, with receiving candidates for supervision. This jury had to receive the agreement of the trainer, of the supervisor(s), and consider the work. The analyst did not enter into it. The qualification of AE, internal to the community, had to be given (or not) by the admission jury, after the procedure of the *pass*, to those who had chosen to engage, on the basis of their experience, with the work of doctrinal development. The fact that there were two titles, which were not related hierarchically, referring to two different orders, meant that neither one was enough in itself to determine a "being an analyst" which could be "sufficient" (to itself). The AME and the AE both derive from the principle that an analyst only authorizes himself from himself and from the act, but they do not inscribe themselves in the same way in relation to the desire to know something about it. If neither of these titles could make the analyst "sufficient', that is because one can only "be" an analyst on the basis of the supposition instituted by the transference, supposition which one can only sustain because of an initial "un-being" and which will allow an exit from the transference.

Lacan's *Proposition* thus gives the choice to analysts of how to position themselves in relation to analysis and the community of analysts. The School qualified someone by evaluating this choice, rather than, like traditional selection, making the choice for them. In this orientation, Lacan was taught by his experience as a trainer, by the experience of the two splits, by his choices in his practice which made him a heretic in relation to an orthopraxis, by the choice made by analysts who preferred a teaching which developed what analysis might be to an institution preoccupied with its conformity to a standard. AMEs and AEs would therefore be qualified on the basis of a choice, their own. It is a choice with consequences, for to start off with the figure of a founder, necessarily paternal, designated by the title of AME, or with the act as basis for an invention (of a knowledge, a mechanism) designated by the title AE, does not have the same effects and does not invoke the same authority. In 1974, Lacan questioned the logical conditions which would allow an analyst to really have the choice, authorizing himself from himself and a few others, to position himself in one way or another to analysis. If the writing of the formulas of sexuation implies that a speaking being authorizes himself from himself and from the necessarily contingent encounter with some other(s), in order to inscribe himself in relation to the phallic function and castration as man or woman, the writing is missing which would allow the analyst to truly have the choice to inscribe himself in one way or another in relation to the "function" which determines him. At the same time, Lacan was ironic about the cipher of the soul (*ame*) constituted by the AME, noted the ravages effected by a "naming" on play when one is given a title to a function, and proposed to three Italian analysts to form a school simply by "naming" an AE when there was one. He let it be understood in his letter that the experience of a School that his *Proposition* had tried to found was not quite it.

Yet, there lies the key to the qualification that Lacan's *Proposition* aimed at: to take the risk of saying "that's it", and to name it. It is the key to of the institution of analysis as lay, in which analysis and the analyst are characterized by a symbolic determination of the act which underlies practice and not by referring to some order of transmission, sacred, paternal, or initiatory. In this sense, it is not certain that the qualification of professional competence established following a hierarchical order is sufficient to qualify analysis as lay for "the outside world". The key to the qualification of AE is to delineate the real, that of the *jouissance* the treatment deals with, but also that of the group and its *jouissance*. Lacan, in effect, tied the nomination of the analyst, which engages the responsibility of the School and thereby gives it being, to the recognition of the real at play in the training, to the choice the analyst can make in recognizing this real and not just cover it with a symptom and a phantasy. To delineate the real engages the two operations of the subject which Freud focused on in the *Ichspaltung*: the "I do not want to know anything about it" of repression and the "I do not want to know anything of it" of negation. Freud said that theory postulates as aim of the treatment the retroactive correction of the processes at the basis of repression. We could add that Lacan's development allows us to postulate that the operation on the object has a corrective aim with respect to negation.

It is not easy to grasp how Lacan tied together the title of AE, the real, and the School, and it is therefore important to see how the question has fared. On 10 November 1963, the General Assembly of the SFP debated the exclusion of Lacan proposed a month earlier by the study commission (Miller, 1977a, pp. 92–103). On the horizon, weighing on the discussion, was the imminent rupture of the negotiations with the IPA and the risk of a split within the SFP. That is when Aubry questioned the title of analyst with respect to its function:

> Is it possible to function as analyst without this title? ... Will we only be analysts when we are recognised by others, "named analysts", or will we be so because we recognise ourselves to be such from within? It seems to be the case that in the analytic relation at any rate, the analyst is recognised as such by the analysand and by himself.

The context led her to refer the imminent separation to another horizon, only twenty years previously, and probably still current for many: the facts of the past war showed that the international backing of the IPA allowed analysts such as Freud, Spitz, and Loewenstein to "avoid the most degrading experiences. Is it only the IPA that can provide such support?"

It is difficult to find a more compelling reason for keeping the shelter that the title of psychoanalyst can provide. Lacan made an effort to make the School such a "shelter", but not at the cost of diminishing the "duties implicated in the desire of the analyst". At the horizon of his *Proposition* he does, therefore, mention what an efficient response the IPA was for the Jewish analysts of *Mitteleuropa* who were recognized, "named analyst", by it. It suggests that the School, in its duty to recognize the real active in the training, had to guide itself with this response to the real that the title of analyst, the name analyst, constitutes. But there was a gap between the answer of exile that the IPA facilitated in most cases and Lacan's *Proposition*: the irreducible fracture of the Shoah and the structural real of humanity it laid bare. This trauma, in which the horror of "selection" resonated, poses a question to each analyst, and also to the institution, the question of Anne-Lise Stern: "What analysis after Auschwitz?" (Stern, 1999). To fence off this hole with the signifiers of *lalangue* does not reduce it. The invention of the mechanism of the *pass*, connected to the invention of the object little *a*, testifies to Lacan's understanding of this question, which joined the question that had been his own since the end of the war.

With his *Proposition*, Lacan invented an apparatus the real of which allowed a recognition of the real through which the analyst was trained. Similarly, he developed the real at play when, weaving the signifiers of *lalangue*, their efflorescence is reduced to the inaugural signifier of repetition and the "object" part of the being of the subject is uncovered. This lost remainder of the signifying articulation makes up the radical alterity of the "self" that the subject aspires to refind and its incommensurability with the signifier. That "self" perceived as agalma in the phantasy, at once a marvel and a reject dropped from the desire of the parents, is only approached at the cost of a subjective destitution which makes one "be" more strongly and confronts one with the real of enjoyment, which exceeds the symbolic. Through his choice of a position within structure, the subject has organized a certain relation to this real and he seeks in the ordinary passions of love, hate, and ignorance a way of realizing this being while protecting himself from it by means of the phantasy. The transference, because it presupposes a subject for this unconscious knowledge, by means of the love and hate addressed to it, crystallizes these three passions. Yet, it is the way analysis can offer desire a chance of finding its source in "unbeing". The relation of the subject to the real can be altered after this, the passion of the transference, which "runs through" the unconscious, can be undone by it. Already, in 1953, Lacan held that in recognizing the limits of the experience but obfuscating the initial positions of the subject, selection missed the fact that if "analysis changes nothing in the real . . . it does change everything for the subject" (Lacan, 1982). It thereby prevents an explanation how and with what it operates on the subject besides the transference: with the desire of the analyst. There we have an aim of the apparatus of the *pass*: to explain, and first of all for the *passant* himself, how the treatment has worked to the point of giving a chance to the object little *a*, for example by offering to another the chance of repeating the operation. That is one result among others for the desire formed there and which is not subsumed in one's professional status, which covers it rather than being based on it. By keeping this gap between a didactic result and professional status, Lacan envisaged that an analysis could one day "be demanded for training purposes even if there was no wish to set up in the profession" (Lacan, 1970a, p. 20).

To transmit how the function of the impossible operated in the apparatus of the treatment, by means of the transference, on the relation of the subject to the impossible, exceeds any direct transmission (interview, writing, lecture, etc.). Lacan considered that the logical development he made of it was not enough either for this transmission and that neither the treatment nor supervision nor the cartel were right for making this knowledge exist. It needed an apparatus that could touch this impossible through its very structure. Putting the drive objects, as real, to work by means of the indirect testimony (suspension of the voice and look of the *passant*), the gap left between what the *passant* said and his saying it, the fact of confiding the transmission of the saying to the *passeurs* who are closest to its truth, the division of the function of *passeur* between two *passeurs*: this real of the apparatus allows one to touch the real with which the analyst trained, to "reach" the act "through the way in which it lodges itself in the agent (*ibid.*, p. 13). This permits the "passing" analyst to use, not the act, which is still beyond him, but his "relation to the act". It allows the analysts who are supposed to have forgotten it to re-experience this moment enough for them to say "that's it", in naming it.

When an analyst attempts to convey with this apparatus how, in the maze of the work of the unconscious and the transference, the desire of the analyst was formed, it has effects of training for all concerned. The experience undergone in this apparatus is a privileged way of working the double movement of subjectivization and objectivization of knowledge which renders possible a non-dogmatic and non-phantasmatic relation to doctrine and one which is not just a rehashing of it. It allows one to pass via the way of the "most particular of the subject", where each case puts analytic science into question. It allows one to pass via the way of that enunciation situated in the edge between truth and knowledge. The apparatus is not just there to verify and authenticate, according to the current terms, the *pass* happening in the treatment. It allows a teaching experience of what the treatment has taught, in which one can circumscribe closely what is lacking in what is said and in what is known. If the telling of the *pass*, transmitted by the *passeurs*, has effects of training, it can shed light on a strange comment of Lacan's. In the first version of his *Proposition*, he said that the AE had "the same position as what one calls elsewhere a trainer", and that he had said since 1964 that an analyst is only a trainer in the *après-coup* of a particular treatment which trained an analyst, without prejudging the outcome of any other treatment. That the *pass* of an AE has, because of the apparatus, effects of training, first of all training him as Analyst of the School, does not give him membership to any body, not even that of the School for which he accepts becoming responsible with others. This is doubtless because, in that experience, he has taken stock of his debt towards analysis.

In its very precariousness, the experience of each party in the *pass* forms a novel working bond, made up of articulating to some others how each analyst has knitted together the work of the unconscious and the work of theory. This link to some others brings with it a relation to otherness made possible by the subject's separation from his "self" and by the precipitation of pure difference that results from it. It also implies another necessity for the institution in addition to its doctrinal and social necessity. That an analyst in this apparatus commits to a reading of the act, that he considers that the very private co-ordinates of this act belong to the "common good", on condition of a development and for a public defined by the apparatus, that other analysts can hear this and risk themselves in naming that *something of* an analyst has been "trained", inscribes a link between analysts which does not derive from either transference, prestige, or genealogy. The knotting of experience and knowledge in a community of encounters, which does not constitute a rapport, can contribute to the formation of the School. This training, created from a pooling together, governed by the apparatus of the *pass*, of what is without common measure, has to recognize the modality of the encounter which constitutes it: its contingency.

Perspective

They say that Navajo women never complete a tapestry, just as a painter might forget to paint a tiny corner of his canvas. But, if a painter can forget to forget, the women never forget to leave a hole. Because they have woven the cloth with all their heart, they fear that it might remain caught in the stitches.

We have woven some signifiers of the training of the analyst around the hole produced by the splits that, in two stages, separated Lacan from the IPA. We have placed those signifiers in the archaeology and history of the difficult question posed to analysts: does one have to institutionalize the training of an analyst, and if so, how? This putting in perspective reveals two sides to training, which each analyst has to deal with, in relation to which he orientates himself, according to a choice no doubt made in the unconscious. Against an initial prejudice, it seems to us that Lacan had tried to hold together, while distinguishing them, the hierarchical dimension of filiation and the dimension of the act.

We decided not to study the actual situation of training today. Dated and localized, our work is, in fact, determined by the effect of the hole that the dissolution of the Freudian School of Paris has produced, followed soon after by the death of Lacan. The dispersion that followed makes it obvious that the orientation of analysts in relation to the two sides of training does not echo the rift effected by the split. Yet having to situate oneself in relation to these two dimensions concerns the pupils of Lacan as much as the analysts of the IPA, perhaps more in France than elsewhere. The French situation could, therefore, be exemplary. Something remains to be invented that would allow analysts to guide themselves in the training in relation to these two sides and, in the choice they make, to see themselves as partners of those who have chosen the other side. This presupposes that the logics of the training that we have tried to describe are not considered as models to conform to or to reject, nor as ideal types, but as ways of responding to the impossible nature of the profession. These ways of responding are inscribed in a complex way in the history of analytic institutions, for institutionalizing the training of the analyst is attempting the impossible knotting of the three "impossible professions" listed by Freud: analysing, educating, and governing.

To recognize that there are two dimensions to training for each analyst and a possible choice in the way of situating oneself in relation to analysis and the analytic community, is to recognize the otherness of each analyst. A certain trajectory has been accomplished by the SPP since the debates on training at the end of the 1960s and the fusion in 1986 of the Society and the Institute. The modifications to the standard that that Society and the APF brought contributed to putting into question the orthopraxis that made the IPA a technicist bureaucracy. The dispersion of Lacan's students certainly followed the lines of transference links, but, in essence, the bond with his teaching was decisive. The relation to the two apparatuses of the school established by this teaching, in particular the relation to his proposition to rethink the qualification of the analyst, doubtlessly guided this dispersion. From this point of view, we think that the diaspora of Lacan's students started in 1969 with the departure of those analysts who founded the Fourth Group, their name anticipating the fact that it would become necessary to count the groups. We can see in it the sign of a real (the real of number linked to that of a group): to be recognized and treated. The pupils who rejected the proposition of the *pass* have, for the most part, brought back the traditional training and its qualifications, seeking to invent more analytical ways of institutionalizing it; others have denied the institution this responsibility. Among those who have adopted the cartels and the *pass*, the differences remain important; they concern the interpretation of the paradoxical relations between the *pass* and the institution. Some have given up on the nomination of the AE; others have taken up the structure of the School, some using the apparatuses to create "mass transference" while others were thinking up ways of giving a chance to the analytic and institutional stakes of nomination.

We must recognize these differences and appreciate the effects that these interpretations introduce with respect to the aims of the apparatuses and the inventions that they have made possible. One can hypothesize that it would have been necessary, in order to make this recognition possible, to have worked through the traumas and mournings. But the corporatist initiatives of psychotherapists and the inclination of European states towards social control have introduced something of the function of haste into this necessary working through. The schemes to organize the psychotherapy profession have given analysts the occasion and no doubt the duty to declare the particularity of their discipline and their practice, and the implications, for training, of its lay character. Despite the different social, scientific, and medical context, we are in the same situation in which Freud found himself, in 1926, of having to convey to the public authorities the wrong they would do to analysis if they were to subsume it into another profession: medicine in 1926, psychotherapy today. After sixty years of affiliation of American analysis with psychiatry and medicine, one analyst of the American Psychoanalytic Association concluded in 1980 in Broadway that the

APA had to "backtrack", given the threat to its integrity. If analysis cannot keep its tense and paradoxical relation to psychotherapy (which implies that it not be included in it), it would be equally under threat. To make this understood requires that one convey how through its aim of resolving the transference, the practice of analysis contests in the most rigorous way the manipulation and sectarian appropriation of the subject supposed to know. This is not only of concern to the subject, but to civilization itself.

REFERENCES AND BIBLIOGRAPHY

Alexander, F. (1985). The theoretical *cursus*. In: Rapport original sur les dix ans de l'Institut de Berlin, in *On forme des psychanalystes*. Paris: Denoel.
Analytica (1978). Nouveaux documents sur la scission de 1953, No. 7.
Andreas-Salomé, L. (1965). *The Freud Journal of Lou Andreas-Salomé*, S. A. Leavy (Trans.). London: Hogarth.
Andreas-Salomé, L. (1991). *Looking Back: Memoirs*, B. Mitchel (Trans.). New York: Paragon.
Aubry, J., Klotz, H. P., Lacan, J., Raimbault, G., Royer, P., & Wolf, L. M. (1966). La place de la psychanalyse dans la médecine. *Cahiers du Collège de médecine, 7*: 761–777.
Balint, M. (1948). On the psychoanalytic training system. *International Journal of Psycho-Analysis, 29*: 163–173 [reprinted in: *Primary Love and Psychoanalytic Technique*, London: Karnac, 1985].
Balint, M. (1952). *Primary Love and Psycho-Analytic Technique*. London: Karnac, 1985.
Balmès, F. (1999). *Ce que Lacan dit de l'être*. Paris: PUF.
Bernfeld, S. (1962). On psychoanalytic training. *Psychoanalytic Quarterly, 31*: 453–482.
Brainin, E., & Kaminer, I. J. (1982). Psychanalyse et national-socialisme. In: Psyché, A.-L. Stern (Trans.) in *L'Écrit du Temps*. Paris: Minuit, 1984.

Braud, A.-M. (1998). Effets de présentation. *Essaim*, 2.
Canguilhem, G. (1968). Qu'est-ce que la psychologie? In: *Études d'histoire de la philosophie des sciences*. Paris: Vrin.
Castelli, E. (1964). Ce sont deux choses hétérogènes. *Tecnica e Casuistica*, Padova.
Clavreul, J. (1978). *L'Ordre médical*. Paris: Seuil.
Costecalde, A., Gárate-Martinez, I., Lachaud, D., & Trono, C. (1995). *Devenir psychanalyste. Les formations de l'inconscient*. Paris: Denoël.
Czermak, M. (1987). L'enseignement de la présentation des malades de Jacques Lacan à Henri-Rousselle. *Bulletin de l'Association freudienne*, 23.
Detienne, M. (1999) [1967]. *The Masters of Truth in Archaic Greece*, J. Lloyd (Trans.). New York: Zone Books.
Donnet, J.-L. (1969). Cursus et hiérarchie dans la société d'analyse. Esquisse d'une étude structurale. *Études freudiennes*, 1–2: 111–150.
Eitingon, M. (1923). Report on the Berlin Psycho-Analytical Policlinic, March 1920–June 1922. *International Journal of Psycho-Analysis*, 4: 254–269.
Eitingon, M. (1926). Announcement during 9th Congress in Bad Homburg in 1925. *Bulletin of the IPA*, 7: 130–135.
Eitingon, M. (1929). Report of 30th July 1929. *International Journal of Psycho-Analysis*, 10.
Erasmus, D. (1993). *Praise of Folly*, B. Radice (Trans.). London: Penguin Classics.
Fabre, M. (1994). *Penser la formation*. Paris: PUF.
Falzeder, E. (Ed.) (2002). *The Complete Correspondence of Sigmund Freud and Karl Abraham 1907–1925*, C. Schwarzacher (Trans.). London: Karnac.
Falzeder, E., & Brabant, E. (Ed.) (1996). *The Correspondence of Sigmund Freud and Sándor Ferenczi 1908–1933*, 3 Vols, P. T. Hoffer (Trans.). Cambridge, MA: Belknap Press of Harvard.
Ferenczi, S. (1955). The elasticity of the psycho-analytical technique. In: *Final Contributions to the Problems and Methods of Psycho-Analysis* (pp. 87–101). London: Hogarth.
Ferenczi, S. (1968–1982). *Psychanalyse: Oeuvres complètes* (4 volumes). Paris: Payot.
Ferenczi, S. (1982). The problem of the end of analysis. In: *Psychanalyse, IV, OC* (pp. 43–52. Paris: Payot.
Ferenczi, S., & Rank, O. (1956). *The Development of Psychoanalysis*, C. Newton (Trans.). New York: Dover.

Fondation européenne pour la psychanalyse (1995). *La Formation des psychanalystes*. Paris: Point hors ligne.
Foucault, M. (1961). *History of Madness in the Classical Age*, J. Khalfa & J. Murphy (Trans.). London: Routledge, 2006.
Foucault, M. (1997). Entrevue avec Michel Foucault. *Ornicar?*, *10*: 62–93.
Foucault, M. (1998) [1976]. *The History of Sexuality: Vol. 1: The Will to Knowledge*, R. Hurley (Trans.). London: Penguin.
Freud, S. (1901a). On dreams. *S.E.*, *5*: London: Hogarth.
Freud, S. (1904a). Freud's psycho-analytic procedure. *S.E.*, *7*: 249–256. London: Hogarth.
Freud, S. (1905a). On psychotherapy. *S.E.*, *7*: 257–270. London: Hogarth.
Freud, S. (1905e). *Fragment of an Analysis of a Case of Hysteria. S.E.*, *7*: 3–122. London: Hogarth.
Freud, S. (1910d). The future prospects of psycho-analytical therapy. *S.E.*, *11*: London: Hogarth.
Freud, S. (1911e). The handling of dream-interpretation in psycho-analysis. *S.E.*, *12*: 89–96. London: Hogarth.
Freud, S. (1912b). The dynamics of transference. *S.E.*, *12*: 97–108. London: Hogarth.
Freud, S. (1912e). Recommendations to physicians practising psycho-analysis. *S.E.*, *12*: 109–120. London: Hogarth.
Freud, S. (1913c). On beginning the treatment. *S.E.*, *12*: 121–144. London: Hogarth.
Freud, S. (1914d). On the history of the psycho-analytic movement. *S.E.*, *14*: London: Hogarth.
Freud, S. (1914g). Remembering, repeating and working-through. *S.E.*, *12*: 145–156. London: Hogarth.
Freud, S. (1915a). Observations on transference-love. *S.E.*, *12*: 157–170. London: Hogarth.
Freud, S. (1915–1917). *Introductory Lectures on Psycho-Analysis. S.E.*, *15–16*: London: Hogarth.
Freud, S. (1919a). Lines of advance in psycho-analytic therapy. *S.E.*, *17*: London: Hogarth.
Freud, S. (1919d). Introduction to psycho-analysis and the war neurosis. *S.E.*, *17*: London: Hogarth.
Freud, S. (1919e). "A child is being beaten" . . . *S.E.*, *17*: 175–203. London: Hogarth.
Freud, S. (1919j). On teaching psycho-analysis in universities. *S.E.*, *17*: London: Hogarth.
Freud, S. (1920c). Dr. Anton von Freund. *S.E.*, *18*: London: Hogarth.

Freud, S. (1920g). *Beyond the Pleasure Principle*. S.E., 18: 7–64: London: Hogarth.
Freud, S. (1921c). *Group Psychology and the Analysis of the Ego*. S.E., 18: London: Hogarth.
Freud, S. (1926e). *The Question of Lay Analysis*. S.E., 20: London: Hogarth.
Freud, S. (1926i). Dr. Reik and the problem of quackery. S.E., 21: London: Hogarth.
Freud, S. (1937c). *Analysis Terminable and Interminable*. S.E., 23: 216–253. London: Hogarth.
Freud, S. (1939a). *Moses and Monotheism*. S.E., 23: London: Hogarth.
Freud, S. (1940a). *An Outline of Psycho-Analysis*. S.E., 23: London: Hogarth.
Freud, S., & Pfister, O. (1963). *Psychoanalysis and Faith: The Letters of Sigmund Freud and Oskar Pfister*. New York: Basic Books.
Gagey, J., & Gagey, J.-M. (1990). La casuistique. *Histoires de cas, Nouvelle Revue de psychanalyse*, 42: 261–284.
Gitelson, M. (1954). The therapeutic problems in the analysis of the "normal" candidate. *International Journal of Psychoanalysis*, 35(II): 174–183.
Glover, E. (1955). *The Technique of Psychoanalysis*. New York: International Universities Press.
Goldstein, J. (1997). *Consoler et classifier, l'essor de la psychiatrie française*. Institut Synthélabo pour le progrès de la connaissance.
Goodman, S. (1982). De la sélection. In: S. Lebovici & A. Solnit (Eds.), *La Formation du psychanalyste* (pp. 171–193). Paris: PUF.
Grubrich-Simitis, I. (1997). *Back to Freud's Texts: Making Silent Documents Speak*, P. Slotkin (Trans.). New Haven, CT: Yale University Press.
Hegel, G. W. F. (1979). *Phenomenology of Spirit*, A. V. Miller (Trans.). Oxford: Oxford University Press.
Heidegger, M. (1958). *Essais et conférences*, A. Preau (Trans.). Paris: Gallimard.
Heidegger, M. (1977). *The Question Concerning Technology, and Other Essays*, W. Lovitt (Trans.). New York: Harper & Row.
Hinshelwood, R. D. (1995). Le mythe du compromis britannique: reflexions sur les dissensions au sein de la Société Britannique de psychanalyse. *Topique*, 57: 229–244.
Horney, K. (1985). On organisation: in Rapport original sur les dix ans de l'Institut de Berlin, in *On forme des psychanalystes* (pp. 125–134). Paris: Denoel.

Jones, E. (1957). *Sigmund Freud: Life and Work*, Volume 3. London: Hogarth, 1980.

Kaufmann, P. (Ed.) (1998). *L'Apport freudien. Éléments pour une encyclopédie de la psychanalyse*. Paris: Larousse-Bordas.

King, P. (1981). The education of a psycho-analyst. *Scientific Bulletin, The British Psychoanalytical Society*, February: 1–20.

Knight, R. P. (1953). The present status of organized psychoanalysis in the United States. *Journal of the American Psychoanalytic Association*, 1(2): 197–221.

Kovacs, V. (1936). Training and control analysis. *International Journal of Psychoanalysis*, 17: 346–54. Published in French by M. Moreau with the 1937 Report of the International Training Committee in his article 'Analyse quatrième, contrôle, formation' *Topique*, no. 18, 1977.

Lacan, J. (1932). *De La Psychose paranoïaque dans ses rapports avec la personnalité*. Paris: Seuil, 1975.

Lacan, J. (1947). La psychiatrie anglaise et la guerre. *L'évolution psychiatrique*, 1: 293–312 & 313–318; in *Autres Écrits* (pp. 101–120).

Lacan, J. (1957). La psychanalyse et son enseignement. *Bulletin de la Société française de philosophie*, pp. 65–85.

Lacan, J. (1965). Acte de fondation, Note adjointe, Préambule. *Annuaire de l'École Freudienne de Paris*. Also in *Autres Écrits* (pp. 229–241). Paris: Seuil, 2001.

Lacan, J. (1966). *Écrits*. Paris: Seuil.

Lacan, J. (1968a). Raison d'un échec. *Scilicet, 1*; in *Autres Écrits* (pp. 341–350).

Lacan, J. (1968b). Proposition du 9 octobre 1967 sur le psychanalyste de l'École. *Scilicet, 1*; in *Autres Écrits* (pp. 243–260).

Lacan, J. (1970a). Discours prononcé par J. Lacan le 6 décembre 1967 à l'EFP. *Scilicet, 2–3*; in *Autres Écrits* (pp. 261–282).

Lacan, J. (1970b). Liminaire. *Scilicet, 2–3*.

Lacan, J. (1970c). *Lettres de l'EFP, 7*.

Lacan, J. (1973). L'Étourdit. *Scilicet, 4*; in *Autres Écrits* (pp. 449–496).

Lacan, J. (1975a). *De la Psychose paranoïaque dans ses rapports avec la personnalité*. Paris: Seuil.

Lacan, J. (1975b). . . . Ou pire. *Scilicet, 5*; in *Autres Écrits* (pp. 547–552).

Lacan, J. (1975–1976). *Le Séminaire, Livre XXIII, Le Sinthome*. Paris: Seuil, 2005.

Lacan, J. (1976). Conferences and lectures in American universities. *Scilicet, 6–7*: 7–63.

Lacan, J. (1977). Sur l'expérience de la passe, 3rd November 1973. *Ornicar?, 12–13*.

Lacan, J. (1982). SFP Conference: "Le symbolique, l'imaginaire et le réel", 8th July 1953, *Bulletin de l'Association freudienne*, 1.
Lacan, J. (1986). Le nombre treize et la forme logique de la suspicion. *Ornicar?*, 36; in *Autres Écrits* (pp. 85–100).
Lacan, J. (1990a). *The Seminar Book I, Freud's Papers on Technique*, J. Forrester (Trans.). New York: W. W. Norton.
Lacan, J. (1990b). *The Seminar, Book II, The Ego in Freud's Theory and in the Technique of Psychoanalysis*, S. Tomaselli (Trans.). New York: W. W. Norton.
Lacan, J. (1990c). *Television: A Challenge to the Psychoanalytic Establishment*, translated by D. Hollier, R. Krauss, & A. Michelson, London: W. W. Norton.
Lacan, J. (1991). *The Seminar of J. Lacan, Book XI, The Four Fundamental Concepts of Psychoanalysis*, A. Sheridan (Trans.). London: Penguin.
Lacan, J. (1999). *The Seminar of J. Lacan, Book VII: The Ethics of Psychoanalysis*, 1959–1960, J.-A. Miller (Ed.), D. Porter, (Trans.). London: Routledge.
Lacan, J. (2000). *The Seminar, Book XX, On Feminine Sexuality, The Limits of Love and Knowledge*, Bruce Fink (Trans.) London: W. W Norton.
Lacan, J. (2001). Allocution de clôture du Congrès sur l'enseignement. In: *Autres Écrits* (pp. 297–305). Paris: Seuil.
Lacan, J. (2006a). Presentation on transference. In: *Écrits: The First Complete English Edition* (pp. 176–185), B. Fink (Trans.). London: W. W. Norton.
Lacan, J. (2006b). Variations on the standard treatment. In: *Ecrits: The First Complete English Edition* (pp. 269–302), B. Fink (Trans.). London: W. W. Norton.
Lacan, J. (2006c). The function and field of speech and language in psychoanalysis. *Ecrits: The First Complete English Edition* (pp. 197–268), B. Fink (Trans.). London: W. W. Norton.
Lacan, J. (2006d). Beyond the "reality principle". In: *Ecrits: The First Complete English Edition* (pp. 58–74), B. Fink (Trans.). London: W. W. Norton.
Lacan, J. (2006e). Logical time and the assertion of anticipated certainty. In: *Ecrits: The First Complete English Edition* (pp. 161–175), B. Fink (Trans.). London: W. W. Norton.
Lacan, J. (2006f). The mirror stage as formative of the *I* function. In: *Ecrits: The First Complete English Edition* (pp. 75–82), B. Fink (Trans.). London: W. W. Norton.

Lacan, J. (2006g). Presentation on psychical causality. In: *Écrits: The First Complete English Edition* (pp. 123–160), B. Fink (Trans.). London: W. W. Norton.
Lacan, J. (2006h). Science and truth. In: *Écrits: The First Complete English Edition* (pp. 726–745), B. Fink (Trans.). London: W. W. Norton.
Lacan, J. (2006i). On Freud's "Trieb" and the psychoanalyst's desire. In: *Écrits: The First Complete English Edition* (pp. 722–725), B. Fink (Trans.). London: W. W. Norton.
Lacan, J. (2006j). On a question prior to any possible treatment of psychosis. In: *Écrits: The First Complete English Edition* (pp. 445–488), B. Fink (Trans.). London: W. W. Norton.
Lacan, J. (2006k). The situation of psychoanalysis and the training of psychoanalysts in 1956. In: *Écrits: The First Complete English Edition* (pp. 384–411), B. Fink (Trans.). London: W. W. Norton.
Lacan, J. (2007). *The Seminar, Book XVII, The Other Side of Psychoanalysis*, R. Grigg (Trans.). London: W. W. Norton.
Le Brun, J. (1998). Expérience, travail, critique. *Cahiers pour une école*, 1.
Le Brun, J. (2000). Sur les notions de hiérarchie et de *gradus*. *Essaim*, 6.
Le Brun, J. (2004). *La jouissance et le trouble* (pp. 67–89). Genève: Droz.
Lebovici, S., & Solnit, A. (Eds.) (1982). *La Formation du psychanalyste*. Paris: PUF.
Leclaire, S., & l'APUI (1991). *États des lieux de la psychanalyse*. Paris: Albin Michel.
Mannoni, M. (1976). *Un lieu pour vivre*. Paris: Seuil.
Mannoni, M. (1984). Enfance aliénée. In: *L'Espace analytique*. Paris: Denoël.
Miller, J.-A. (Ed.) (1976). La scission de 1953. *Ornicar?*, 12(Suppl.).
Miller, J.-A. (1977a). L'excommunication. *Ornicar?*, 8(Suppl.).
Miller, J.-A. (1977b). Enseignement de la présentation des malades. *Ornicar?*, 10.
Milner, J.-C. (1995). *L'Œuvre Claire*. Paris: Seuil.
Nacht, S., Lebovici, S., & Diatkine, R. (1960). L'enseignement de la psychanalyse. *Revue française de psychanalyse*, XXIV: 225–240.
Nassif, J. (1999). *Comment devient-on psychanalyste?* Ramonville Saint-Agne: Érès.
Nawawi, C. (1999). Écritures lacaniennes. *Carnets de l'EPSF*, 26–27.
Paskaukas, R. A. (Ed.) (1993). *The Complete Correspondence of Sigmund Freud and Ernest Jones 1908–1939*. Cambridge, MA: Belknap of Harvard University Press.

Pfeiffer, E. (Ed.) (1966). *Sigmund Freud and Lou Andreas-Salomé: Letters*, W. Robson-Scott & E. Robson-Scott (Trans.). London: Hogarth, 1972.
Porge, E. (1985). La présentation des malades. *Littoral, 17*.
Porge, E. (1989). *Se compter trois. Le temps logique de Lacan*. Toulouse: Érès.
Radó, S. (1985). The practical *cursus*. In: Rapport original sur les dix ans de l'Institut de Berlin, in *On forme des psychanalystes*, Paris: Denoel.
Rank, O. (1929). *The Trauma of Birth*. New York: Harcourt Brace.
Reik, T. (1953). *The Haunting Melody: Psychoanalytic Experiences in Life and Music*. New York: Farrar, Straus & Young.
Revue Littoral (1992). *Ecritures lacaniennes*, No. 36.
Roudinesco, E. (1982–1986). *La Bataille de cent ans. Histoire de la psychanalyse en France*, Vol. 2. Paris: Seuil.
Roudinesco, E. (1990). *Jacques Lacan & Co. A History of Psychoanalysis in France, 1925–1985*, J. Mehlman (Trans.). London: Free Association Books.
Roudinesco, E., & Plon, M. (1997). *Dictionnaire de la psychanalyse*. Paris: Fayard.
Sachs, H. (1939). The prospects of psycho-analysis. *International Journal of Psycho-Analysis, 20*: 460–464.
Sachs, H. (1945). *Freud, Master and Friend*. London: Imago.
Sachs, H. (1947). Observations of a training analyst. *Psychoanalytic Quarterly, 16*: 157–168.
Sachs, H. (1985). In: Rapport original sur les dix ans de l'Institut de Berlin, in *On forme des psychanalystes*, Paris: Denoel.
Safouan, M. (1983). *Jacques Lacan et la question de la formation des analystes*. Paris: Seuil. English edition: *Jacques Lacan and the Question of Psychoanalytic Training*, J. Rose (Trans.). New York: St. Martin's Press, 2000.
Safouan, M., Julien, P., & Hoffmann, C. (1995). *Malaise dans la psychanalyse. Le tiers dans l'institution et l'analyse de contrôle*. Paris: Arcanes.
Scarpalezou, A. (1995). Note sur le cartel. *Carnets de l'École de psychanalyse Sigmund Freud, 4*.
Schröter, M. (1996). Zur Frühgeschichte der Laienanalyse. Strukturen eines Kernkonflikts der Freud-Schule. *Psyche, 12*: 1127–1175. Summarised in French by F. Samson. In: *Essaim* (Vol. 1). Ramonville Saint-Agnes: Érès, 1998.
Shengold, L. (1980). De la progression. In: *La Formation du psychanalyste*, Broadway Symposium.

Stein, C. (1977). Sur la pratique des cures contrôlées. In: *La Mort d'Œdipe* (pp. 231–249). Paris: Denoël.
Stern, A.-L. (1998). Sois déportée ... et témoigne! Psychanalyser, témoigner: *double bind? Carnets de L'École de psychanalyse Sigmund Freud, 18*.
Stern, A.-L. (1999). Psychanalyste après Auschwitz? *Essaim, 4*.
Tardits, A. (1998). Communauté d'expérience, communauté de savoir. *Essaim, 1*.
Thompson, N. L. (1995). Les schismes dans le mouvement psychanalytique aux Etats-Unis. *Topique, 57*: 257–270. Reprinted in: É. Roudinesco & M. Plon, (Eds.), *Dictionnaire de la psychanalyse*. Paris: Fayard, 1997.
Valabrega, J. P. (1994). *La Formation du psychanalyste*. Paris: Payot.
Weiss, E. (1970). *Sigmund Freud as a Consultant. Recollections of a Pioneer in Psychoanalysis*, E. Grotjahn (Trans.). New York: Intercontinental Medical Book.
Wittenberg, G., & Tögel, Ch. (1913–1920). *Die Rundbriefe des "Geheimen Komitees"*, Band 1. Tübingen: Diskord, 1999.
Zehn Jahre Berliner psychoanalytisches Institut [Ten Years of the Berlin Psychoanalytic Institute] (1930). Wien: International Psychoanalytical Verlag. French translation: Rapport original sur les dix ans de l'Institut de Berlin, in *On forme des psychanalystes*, Paris: Denoel, 1985.

INDEX

Abraham, K., 8, 14–15, 17, 19, 26–27, 32–35, 38, 72–73
Adler, A., 3, 4, 7, 47, 50
Alexander, F., 19, 32–33, 43, 151
ambivalence, 23, 31, 131
American Psychoanalytic Association, 149–150
Analytica, 57, 151
Andreas-Salomé, L., 1–7, 11, 25, 29, 34, 46–48, 134, 151
anxiety, 14, 73, 77, 110
Anzieu, D., 128
Aristotle, 70, 81
Aubry, J., 102, 105, 144, 151
autonomy, 9, 59, 87, 97

Balint, M., 19, 52–54, 58, 108, 116, 141, 151
Balmès, F., 81, 95, 99, 151
Baty, G., 128
Berlin Institute, 14, 27
Berlin Psychoanalytic Training Institute (Polyclinic), 19–23, 26–27, 32–33, 36
Bernard, C., 68
Bernfeld, S., 23, 33, 53–54, 58–59, 71, 151

Bion, W. R., 128
Blanchot, M., 94
Bleuler, E., 26
Boehm, F. J., 33
Bonneval Congresses, 77, 103
Borromean knot, 97–98, 112
Bourbaki, N., 132
Bouvet, M., 73
Brabant, E., 8, 11–12, 15–18, 48, 152
Brainin, E., 77, 151
Braud, A.-M., 105, 152
British Psychoanalytical Society, 52
Budapest Conference, 14–15, 20
Budapest Congress, 12, 27
Buffon, G. L., 113
Burghölzli Clinic, 26

Canguilhem, G., 80, 152
cases/studies
    Aimée, 101
    Dora, 29, 35, 72
    Irma, 7
    Leonardo da Vinci, 26
Castelli, E., 82, 152
castration, 73, 97, 109–111, 143
    complex, 108, 110
Charcot, J. M., 105

161

Circle of Psychiatric Studies, 104
Claudel, P., 93
Clavreul, J., 24, 152
College of Physicians, 8, 28
countertransference, 8, 53, 74, 80
  see also: transference
Czermak, M., 105, 152
de Certeau, M., xi
de Clérambault, L. N., 113
death, 14, 41, 43, 96–98, 106, 110
drive, ix, 33, 35, 78, 96, 109, 112
Descartes, R., 97, 103
Detienne, M., 80, 152
Diatkine, R., 112, 157
Dolto, F., 81, 105,
Donnet, J.-L., 136, 152
dream(s), 5–10, 21, 26, 30, 33, 48, 87, 99
Dullin, C., 128
Duras, M., 94
During, A., 38

École Freudienne de Paris (EFP), x,
  60, 84, 86, 88–89, 91, 103–104,
  112, 114, 116–117, 120–121,
  124–125, 132, 139, 148
  analyst of (AE), 135, 139–143,
    146–147, 149
  analyst member of (AME), 116,
    139–143
École Pratique des Hautes Études, 131
ego, x, 4, 14, 42, 53, 70, 74–75, 78, 96,
  98, 106, 109–110, 122, 133
  super, x, 40, 53, 74, 116
Eitingon, M., 14–15, 18–25, 33–34,
  37, 47–49, 51, 69–70, 116, 152
Erasmus, D., 87, 94–95, 152
Experimental School of Bonneuil,
  104
Ey, H., 73, 103–104, 113, 121

Fabre, M., 70, 152
Falzeder, E., 8, 11–18, 26–27, 35, 48,
  152
Fénelon, F., 38
Fenichel, O., 21–22, 32–33
Ferenczi, S., 6, 8, 10, 12, 14–16, 18–19,
  21, 32, 39, 48–49, 53, 55–56,

72–73, 76, 107–110, 115, 134, 152
First World War, 12, 77
Fliess, W., 3
Foucault, M., 47, 94, 98, 103,
  125–126, 153
free association, 7, 21, 100
French Society of Psychoanalysis
  (SFP), 67–68, 75, 81–83, 103,
  139, 143–144
Freud, A., 2, 39–40, 50, 52
Freud, S., ix, xi, 1–56, 58–62, 67–69,
  71–74, 76, 78, 81, 83–88, 92–94,
  96, 98–102, 104–112, 114–115,
  122–128, 130, 132, 134, 138,
  143–144, 148–149, 153–154
Freudian orthodoxy, 56–57, 83
Freudian School of Paris *see*: École
  Freudienne de Paris

Gagey, J., 101, 154
Gagey, J.-M., 101, 154
German Psychoanalytic Society, 20,
  25, 35, 56
Gitelson, M., 55, 154
Goldstein, J., 47, 154
Goodman, S., 136–137, 154
Grubrich-Simitis, I., 37, 40, 154

hate, 110, 145
Hegel, G. W. F., 71–72, 123, 154
Heidegger, M., 78–81, 154
Hinshelwood, R. D., 52, 154
Horney, K., 24, 32, 154
Hospital of Sick Children, 102, 105
Hungarian Psychoanalytical
  Association, 43

ignorance, x, 63, 94, 110, 145
Institute of Psychoanalysis, 63, 67
International Psychoanalytic(al)
  Association (IPA), xi, 12, 18,
  50–51, 57–58, 63, 67–68, 70, 72,
  80–82, 85, 87, 106, 112–113, 115,
  122–124, 126, 134, 136–137,
  139–140, 144, 147–148
International Training Committee,
  44–45, 50–51, 68

Internationale Psychoanalytische Vereinigung (IPV), 1, 6, 14, 23, 51
Jones, E., 6, 8, 10, 13, 17, 23, 25, 27, 37, 39–41, 44–45, 47–52, 56, 69, 72–73, 107–108, 115, 121, 134, 155
Jouvet, L., 128
Joyce, J., 94
Jung, C. G., 4, 7, 11–12, 26, 50, 73

Kaminer, I. J., 77, 151
King, P., 52, 155
Klein, M., 19, 52
Klotz, H. P., 102–103, 151
Knight, R. P., 91, 155
Kojève, A., 113
Kovacs, V., 118, 155

La Boétie, E., 133
La Borde clinic, 104
La Salpetrière, 105
Lacan, J., x–xi, 7, 25, 56–63, 65, 68–69, 71–88, 91–114, 116–119, 121–149, 151, 155–157
Lagache, D., 58–59, 67–68, 81
Le Brun, J., 87, 101, 140, 157
Lebovici, S., 64, 112, 157
Leclaire, S., 86
Lévi-Strauss, C., 96
libido, ix, 4, 7, 14, 21, 30
life
   real, 30
   sexual, 98
Loewenstein, R., 61, 68, 144
logical time, 74, 76–77, 84
love, 41, 71, 110, 133, 145
Lukacs, G., 15

Mannoni, M., 104, 128, 157
Miller, J.-A., 56–59, 62, 67–68, 81–82, 105, 143, 157
Milner, J.-C., 96–97, 157
mourning, 87, 108, 149
Müller-Braunschweig, C., 33, 44

Nacht, S., 57–59, 62–64, 67–68, 112, 123, 157

narcissism, 4, 6, 14, 18, 55, 106, 112, 137
Nawawi, C., 97, 157
Nietschze, F., 2
Nunberg, H., 27
Nuremberg Congress, 9, 18

object, 29–30, 56, 74, 76, 81, 88, 99, 101, 103–104, 110–111, 113–114, 117–119, 124, 126–127, 129, 134, 141, 143, 145–146
   little *a*, 82, 94, 97, 110–112, 126–127, 129, 134, 136, 144–145
   negotiated, 82–83
   of analysis, 5–6, 35, 94
objective/objectivity, 2, 8, 51, 55, 70, 78, 84, 87, 125, 128, 146
Oedipus complex, 31, 40, 54, 73, 100
Other, 80, 101, 110–111, 116, 127, 129, 133, 135, 138, 141
Oury, J., 104
Oxford Congress, 51

Paris Psychoanalytical Society, 84
Paskaukas, R. A., 6, 10, 23, 37, 39–40, 45, 49–50, 108, 115, 157
Pfeiffer, E., 2, 7, 13, 14, 25, 29, 134, 158
Pfister, O., 47, 154
phantasy, 31–32, 36, 46, 92, 94, 97, 99, 101, 104, 108–111, 117–118, 122, 124, 126–127, 134, 136, 143, 145–146
Pitoëff, G., 128
Plato, 38, 93
Porge, E., 76, 105, 158
psychic(al)
   apparatus, 32, 40, 96
   factor, 28
   suffering, ix, 46

Radó, S., 15, 19, 33–34, 158
Raimbault, G., 102–103, 151
Rank, O., 11, 21, 51, 72–73, 107, 152, 158
Rée, P., 2
Reik, T., 38–39, 47, 158

repression, ix, 7–8, 11, 31, 35, 41, 46–47, 62, 69, 73, 78, 108–109, 140, 143
resistance, ix, 2, 4, 7, 9, 13–14, 28–29, 31, 33, 35–36, 40–41, 43, 55–56, 63, 69, 74–76, 88, 125, 128, 130, 141
Revue Littoral, 97, 158
Rickman, J., 128
Rilke, R. M., 2
Riviere, J., 50
Roheim, G., 44
Roudinesco, E., 57, 81, 86, 89, 103, 121, 131, 158
Roudinesco, J., 62–64
Rousseau, J. J., 38
Royer, P., 102–103, 151

Sachs, H., 11, 25–27, 30–31, 33, 44, 54, 55–56, 58–59, 158
Safouan, M., xi, 23, 158
Saussure, F., 113
Scarpalezou, A., 128, 158
Schröter, M., 38, 158
Secret Committee, 6, 10–12, 17–18, 23, 51, 53, 72–73, 134, 138
self, 124, 145, 147
  analysis, 6, 9, 11
  authorization, 122, 138
sexuality, ix–x, 14, 40, 42, 92, 94, 125
  infantile, 26, 31
Shakespeare, W., 28, 94
Shengold, L., 112, 158
Simmel, E., 13–15, 19–20, 24, 33, 43
Société Psychanalytique de Paris (SPP), 56–60, 62–63, 75, 112, 136, 139, 148
Sophocles, 94
Spinoza, B., 2, 82–83, 87
Steckel, W., 7
Stein, C., 118, 159
Stern, A.-L., 77, 144, 159
study days, x, 82, 91, 123, 132
subject(s), x, 7, 21, 29, 57, 70–72, 74, 76–77, 80, 82–83, 85, 88, 94–102, 105–107, 110–114, 116–119, 122–127, 129–131, 133, 135, 138, 141, 143, 145–147, 150

subjectivity, 4–5, 7, 28, 33, 77–78, 99, 106–107, 110, 113, 122, 125–129, 145–146
  inter-, 126
symbol(-ism), 20, 33, 74–77, 79, 82, 92–94, 96, 98–100, 104, 106, 132, 138, 141, 143, 145

Tandler, J., 38
Tardits, A., 87, 159
Teaching Commission of the San Francisco Institute, 23–25, 53
Thompson, N. L., 52, 159
Tögel, Ch., 18, 159
transference, ix, 7–8, 11, 14, 21–22, 29–33, 40–41, 43, 46–47, 51, 54, 56, 62, 75–76, 82, 88–89, 93, 97, 100–102, 104–105, 108, 110–112, 115, 118–119, 124, 126–127, 130–131, 137–139, 141–142, 145–150 *see also*: countertransference
trauma, 13–14, 19, 33, 73, 144, 149

unconscious(ness), ix–x, 5, 7, 11, 20–21, 28, 31–32, 40–41, 48, 54–55, 70, 74–75, 82, 88, 92, 94, 96, 98–99, 101, 103, 106–112, 114, 117–118, 125–127, 130–131, 133–135, 145–148

Vienna Psychoanalytic Society, 1–2, 59
Wednesday meetings, 1, 3, 5, 11, 43, 128
von Freund, A., 17–19, 23

Weber, M., 68
Weiss, E., 115, 159
Wiesbaden Congress, 49–51
Wittenberg, G., 18, 159
Wolf, L. M., 102–103, 151
World Congress of Psychiatry, 58

Zehn Jahre Berliner psychoanalytisches Institut (Ten Years of the Berlin Psychoanalytic Institute), 19–20, 22, 159

DATE DUE			

**PROPERTY OF
SOUTH UNIVERSITY LIBRARY
NOVI CAMPUS
NOVI, MI
248-675-0242**

DEMCO